Past and Present

an autobiography

Edward Greenwood

*Best Wishes
for Chris*

The Conrad Press

Past and Present
Published by The Conrad Press in the United Kingdom 2024
Tel: +44(0)1227 472 874
www.theconradpress.com
info@theconradpress.com
ISBN 978-1-916966-43-7
Copyright ©Edward Greenwood 2024
All rights reserved.
Typesetting and Cover Design by: Levellers
The Conrad Press logo was designed by Maria Priestley.
Printed and bound in Great Britain by Clays Ltd, Elcograf S.p.A.

recte calculum ponas ubique nafragium

'If you calculate rightly there is a shipwreck everywhere'.
Petronius, *Satyricon*

1 MY GRANDPARENTS

The task of writing an autobiography is a strange one, because human beings are orientated towards the future. But as the past has conditioned what I am, I cannot become just anything in the future. Some options are open to me and a myriad more are closed.

I cannot become an Athenian hoplite, a soldier in Wellington's army or, thank heavens, a Bolshevik or Nazi. My task is to become what I am in the sense which Nietzsche, following the Greek poet Pindar meant, that is to realize my best potentialities, 'my best self' in Matthew Arnold's words. It will be seen that, like the play *Hamlet,* I am full of quotations. This is because I have always been a reader and a thinker.

In writing an autobiography it is the past which becomes our project. Our task is to deal with what were our past aims, both what conditioned them, and what their outcome was. The roads taken and not taken, so to speak. It is also helpful to take account of previous biographies. I will restrict myself to two. That of St Augustine marks an epoch: the transition from pagan antiquity (he delighted in the Latin poets, especially Virgil) to the Catholic Christian epoch now, thankfully to my mind, come to an end.

It was Augustine who foisted on humanity the appalling doctrine of original sin. As Nietzsche put it in *Daybreak* Christianity 'gave Eros poison to drink.' In

D. H. Lawrence's words it 'did the dirt on sex.' Byron's quip about his account of his sexual activities in his *Confessions* making us envy his transgressions hits the right dismissive tone. For any liberal-minded person, Mill's *Autobiography* will always be rewarding, despite Nietzsche's calling him a 'shallowpate'. His account of how reading Wordsworth's poetry cured him of his depression will always rejoice the heart of anyone interested in literature. John Ruskin's dismal account of the sexual failure of his marriage to Effie Gray shows further the awful effect of Christianity on this central aspect of human life.

My favourite autobiography and my model is Friedrich Nietzsche's *Ecce Homo*. Right from the bold blasphemy of its title, alluding to Pilate's recognition of Jesus, it moves with brio through an account of Nietzsche's works and days. I regard it as the finest autobiography of all, a fit memorial to the man I regard as the greatest philosopher/psychologist who has ever lived.

Today there are organizations which will help you trace your ancestry for centuries back and lay bare your genetic inheritance. But this account will rely on memory and reflections supplemented by such documents as I have to hand.

About my grandparents I know very little. On my mother's side they were the Hesmondhealshes of Clayton-le Moors Lancashire. My maternal grandfather died when I was three, before we moved to a house further along the terrace to 233 Manchester Road, Nelson. I remember him as a distinct and small, but sprightly, figure with white hair and moustache. I believe he was illiterate and had worked as a quarryman. How amazed he would have been to learn that his grandson owns at least 4000 books.

I recall much more about my maternal grandmother for I was five when she died. I was with my mother in the cinema which my father managed (we always got free tickets) watching a Hollywood film when a notice flashed across the screen for us to go home, as there was an emergency. When we got to the house it was to learn from my disconcerted half brother and sister that my grandmother's mouth had suddenly gone all twisted and that she could only make incoherent noises and was behaving very oddly. She had had a stroke. It must have been very frightening for them. Not many days later she died.

As both my parents and my half-sister worked and my half-brother was often away, I had been brought up by the grandmother I had just lost, a white haired gentle and loving soul whom I adored. What I remember best is washing day which always fell on a Monday. The washing was down in the commodious cellar and my job was to pound it in the dolly tub, a task I greatly enjoyed. There was a rumour that rats were to be seen, but the noise of the washing scared them off. There was also an old mangle. My grandmother, as I remember, did much of the cleaning and cooking.

There is a rather sad addendum to this account of my grandmother. This was my first acquaintance with death. It was the custom in those days to exhibit the dead in the coffin for final farewells. I remember being astonished at how cold her brow was when I kissed it. The open coffin was in the front room, the dining room, to the left at the foot of the stairs.

I remember for years having terrifying nightmares that I had to go down the stairs and walk past the room. Suddenly the door would open and something would come out and snatch me into the waiting darkness. All this was no doubt the result of my having seen my grandmother's corpse in there. I was also fearful of the large attic our old, terraced house had. I was sure that it too had a ghost lurking behind the door in the small annex it contained. In these days of comfortable smallish houses, flats and bungalows, there is not the stimulus those old houses gave to the imagination.

2 MY FATHER

My father was a most remarkable person. I don't know anything about his parents, but presumably their surname was Baker as that was given to me as my middle name at baptism. Of middle height and fairly thickset he had been a professional soldier and an amateur boxer in his youth as well as a skilful snooker player. Apparently, he had tried to enter one of the forty or more local spinning or weaving mills in some sort of managerial capacity when he left the army, but had not liked it. He was the friend of a local millionaire called Hartley who owned four cinemas in our small town, Nelson. The millionaire friend made him the manager of one of the four cinemas which he owned. I think it was The Palace. It had been a theatre and had side boxes. It had once staged operas and plays. Many of these theatres were converted to cinemas after the First World War, but some could still put on plays and pantomimes at certain times.

As the millionaire married and founded a family, the better cinemas passed one by one to his sons until my father ended up managing The Alhambra, a tiny cinema in a back street which had, nevertheless, once staged circuses. On visiting my hometown some while ago I discovered the cinema had been burned down because it had become derelict *'Sic Fata Aedificiationibus.'* Such is the fate of so many loved buildings.

It was a great thrill to me when my father let me see the synopses or summaries (the word 'synopsis' fascinated me) of forthcoming films so he could choose those which he thought would best satisfy local taste. This ranged from Hollywood gangster films with James Cagney and Humphrey Bogart, to English films with Stewart Granger and Jean Simmons. There was one daring film, as I recall, in which the latter swam in the nude, her body faintly visible through the waves. My father's cinema would never have countenanced a French film like *La Ronde,* notorious at the time. This scandalised the chapel goers (and there were many) in our local larger neighbouring town, Burnley. It was about promiscuity and had some nude scenes.

In the Alhambra building there was a bin full of sweets and chocolates for distribution in the interval between films, for they usually had two feature films and a newsreel. I was allowed to take a chocolate bar for free. Also inside the building was a room where ice cream was made on a large rolling drum. I was allowed to taste it when it was freshly made. I was also fascinated by the long piston rod and large cylinder of the generator in the basement which supplied the cinema with electricity.

I mentioned the fact that my father had been a regular soldier. As a young lad of fourteen he had been bored with the life in a small provincial mill town where nothing of note ever seemed to happen. Because of this he ran off at the age of fourteen to become a boy soldier. Almost immediately he regretted this. I suspect it was because of the harsh discipline. It was, however, possible for one's family to 'buy one out', as it was called, by paying a sum of money. However his mother is supposed to have made the proverbial remark: 'As you made your bed, so you will lie on it.' There is something typically 'Lancashire' about this story. The Boer war had broken out in South Africa.

Thirsty for adventure, he joined up as a regular in the East Lancashire regiment. The casualties were horrendous, so it was fortunate for him that his battalion was posted to India and not to South Africa. At that time each county regiment had two battalions, one for service at home and the other for service in the Empire.

My father served on the North West Frontier near the famous Khyber Pass. This is where Pakistan and Afghanistan meet. It was feared at the time that the Russians had designs on India and would invade it through Afghanistan, though they found out, as the British had done, that Afghanistan is the graveyard of foreign armies.

3 MY FATHER'S ADVENTURES IN INDIA

I listened entranced to my father's stories of India which I was reminded of when I came to read Rudyard Kipling's stories and especially *The Jungle Book*. Although my father had a distrust of poets and of poetry (which he seemed to regard as an illness) he always excepted Kipling from these strictures.

Everybody seemed to know the famous poem 'Gunga Din' about the *beasti-wallah* or water carrier. My father explained to me the enmity between the mongoose and the cobra which features in a famous story in *The Jungle Book*. He had his own cobra story. One day he had got on his backside to slide down a steep slope when a cobra's menacing pointed head rose up before him with flickering tongue. Its fatal fangs were bared. But he quickly grabbed the rifle he had put down in order to descend the slope and shot it through the head.

He told me tales of the immense noonday heat in India during which the men were confined to barracks and beer. Later I read the consolation of girls was also thoughtfully laid on by the army, but, of course, he did not mention that. He spoke admiringly of the short statured, but very tough, Gurkhas from Nepal with their kukris or curved sharp swords which, he claimed, could behead an opponent at a stroke. He told me of the different religions of India and of the fasting fakirs or holy men. He spoke of the long sticks called *lathis* with which the Indian police used to keep crowds in order. He taught me the Hindi word for 'all right' or 'OK' *'hacha'*. It was in India that he developed a taste for curry with his food. My cousin Ralph, who was in the merchant navy, used to bring back bottles of curry powder for Uncle Ted as he called him. Thus, we enjoyed a delight our fellow countrymen were not to know till decades after.

I suppose my father was eminently what used to be called 'a manly man' in a way I could never be. Before I had to endure the ordeal of boarding school at the age of ten I heard my father expressing his fears for me to my mother. He told her I was too sensitive and that would mean unhappiness. I always felt that so long as he was around I had a sort of protective belt around me wherever I went. However, as he was already fifty when I was born in 1933, I grew anxious about his growing frailty. He had bronchial problems which no doubt stemmed from his long service in the trenches, a story I am coming to. I used to fear his having to discipline the 'roughs' of the town in his cinema, but he always seemed to have everything under control.

4 MY FATHER'S SERVICE IN THE FIRST WORLD WAR.

When, despite the best efforts of the admirable member for Blackburn the Liberal John Morley, Asquith's Liberal cabinet voted for war on Sunday August 4th 1914, my father's regiment, the East Lancashires, immediately entrained and moved to Southampton to embark for Belgium. Only two members of that cabinet had voted against the war. Persuaded by the combative Churchill, despite Morley's best efforts, the once strong pacifist Lloyd George voted with Churchill. Only John Burns, the Labour M.P. voted with Morley. Outside parliament the courageous Ramsay Macdonald of the Labour Party also opposed the war to his great credit. On such decisions did the fate of millions, including that of my father, stand. So my father was one of that noble band Kaiser Wilhelm referred to as 'the old contemptibles'. They were immortalized in poem 37 in A.E. Housman's *Last Poems* 'Epitaph on An Army of Mercenaries'. He refers to them as mercenaries, because unlike the Kitchener's later volunteers, they were regular soldiers on a wage. The famous second and last verse runs

Their shoulders held the sky suspended;
They stood, and earth's foundations stay;
What God abandoned, these defended,
And saved the sum of things for pay.

I used to read Housman to my father and I think Housman, along with Kipling, was one of the few poets he had time for. I don't think he knew Thomas Hardy's poems. At that time poets wrote for the general public and did not just put together obscure collocations of phrases for a coterie of intellectuals.

My son Edward obtained a photocopy of my father's war record from Fulwood Barracks in Preston. I don't know for sure, but I suspect he missed the Battle of Mons, but probably arrived in time for the important holding action at Le Cateau where several men were killed and wounded. The regiment then marched 200 miles due south in thirteen days. The records then show that the battalion pulling back fought actions at Armentieres, Ploegsteert Wood, and, in 1915, at Ypres. So my father must have seen some bitter fighting. As was typical of the soldiers of that terrible war he never spoke about his experiences to me. My mother one told me he had seen young boys crying as they had to march from their billets up to the line and that he had seen many terrible sights. My father was invalided out of the army in January 1916 with trench foot acquired from constantly having to stand in mud and water.

5 MY MOTHER

I was always much closer to my father than to my mother because I spent so much more time with him. The reason for this was that my mother had a well paid job as the manageress (the word was used in those days) of a fur shop in Preston, a large town with a fine civic hall, twenty miles or so to the West. The privations and difficulties of the war years would be incomprehensible to to-day's generation.

There was a total blackout so enemy bombers could not be guided by lights below, and all through that blackout my mother had to travel by bus, with one change, starting about 6a.m. and returning on the 6 o'clock bus at night so she did not get in till about 8pm. My favourite reading at the age of six consisted of the *Beano* and the *Rover* comics which she brought back to me every Thursday. They were eagerly awaited and I was bitterly disappointed if, for some reason, she failed to bring them.

My mother, as I could see from photographs in the main bedroom, had been very beautiful as a girl, fine features, fine figure and lovely dark hair. She had been married to a Welshman with the name Winn and had had two children by him, my half-sister Edith born in 1916 (I will say something later about their difficult relationship) and my half-brother Robert (whom we always called Bobby) born in 1920.

I often wondered if she had been a volunteer auxiliary nurse in the First World War and had met my father when he was convalescing in hospital. I am not sure when her first marriage had broken up. It seems she had a liaison with another man before she met my father, for his name is on the 1916 birth certificate. As to Winn, the name made her deeply suspicious of Welshman all her life.

One of my first memories of my mother comes from when I must have been about three and it is a memory of sexual awakening. I was either in a cradle or in my mother's bed in the main bedroom when I suddenly became aware of her standing naked at my bedside in all her beauty. I had an erection and I recall her pointing at it and laughing. I think this episode makes against rather than for Freud's views, for, on his account, such a memory should have been deeply repressed in the unconscious and only recoverable under analysis.

My mother had a strong constitution which I hope I have inherited. She lived to the age of ninety-two. Mothers often have a fraught relationship with their sons and daughters. The most famous literary account of this is to be found in D.H.Lawrence's novel *Sons and Lovers* in the account of Paul's love for Miriam. Jessie Chambers, the original of Miriam, left a brilliant account of the whole affair in her *D.H. Lawrence: A Personal Record*. Just as mothers want to marry their sons, so they think no man is good enough for their daughters. In the case of Bobby her elder son I can't recollect any young girl to whom he was particularly close and who might have aroused her jealousy. He died at the age of twenty- three serving with Bomber Command. My mother's great love for him came out in her grief at his loss. I will save the account of her interference in her daughter Edith's life for the account of my sister which she follows. Edith was a most gifted and remarkable person.

6 MY HALF-SISTER EDITH

As I have said, Edith was born in 1916. She had a sweet nature and was very clever. She did excellently at Burnley High School for Girls (it has I believe since gone co-ed with the Boys Grammar and may now be a Comprehensive) where, rather unusually for those times, she studied German as well as French. This stood her in good stead later. These days she would have gone to university, but this was a pattern followed by very few then. She did stay on to do Higher School Certificate, but then left school to learn typing and shorthand so she could find work as a secretary.

Here her German came in useful for she worked for Jewish émigrés from Austria and Germany who had founded businesses, first in Nelson and then for Newman's slippers in Blackburn. Much later on, after the Second World War, she went to the University of Keele when it was founded in the 1950's as a mature student and obtained a degree in economics. She afterwards taught the subject in the Girls High School in Newcastle Under Lyme in Staffordshire. She also learned to drive our old Morris Eight. Neither my mother nor my father could drive.

In her early twenties she went through a religious phase. She assiduously attended St Mary's our local Anglican parish church. It was moderately High Anglican and I recall she had a rather sickly picture of the Virgin Mary above her bed in which I sometimes slept when I was around five. We used to play a marvellous game of diving under the sheets.

She claimed there was a wonderful land at the far end. Later we became fascinated by islands, particularly the ones on Lake Borrowdale in the Lake District and imagined how delightful it would be to live on one together. She was very interested in literature. She particularly liked reading Jane Austen and Emily Bronte. She was fascinated by *Wuthering Heights* and loved Emily's mysterious poem 'Cold in the Earth'. I went with her a few times to Howarth which was only about twelve miles away across the Yorkshire Border just beyond Colne, a small neighbouring town named after the Roman colonia that had once been there, just like the German Cologne which was to play such a sad part in our lives. Through wind and rain we struggled across the barren moors in search of the house which was the origin of the 'Wuthering Heights' of the novel as so many admirers of the Brontes have done since. Edith was also knowledgeable about the Lancashire Witches who had been tried at Lancaster Assizes in the early seventeenth century, found guilty and hanged. One of them came from Roughlea, a tiny village not far from Pendle Hill, a whale shaped hill 1800 feet high isolated from the rest of the Pennines. Five miles away, it could easily be seen from our house, a famous landmark. It was a tiring walk to reach and climb on a hot summer's day, but my sister and I did the walk and climb a few times. As I grew older, we both went youth hostelling in the Lake district. My sister was also deeply interested in drama. She wrote nativity plays to be performed by the church at Christmas and was a keen performer in the productions of the local dramatic society.

Her study of German led to an interesting experience. Through correspondence she entered into an exchange with a German girl Greta who came from a small village Wernigerode near the Harz region famous in connection with Goethe's portrayal of the witches in the Walpurgisnacht section of *Faust Part Two*. So it was that Edith set out on her own in August 1934 for Germany.

She could not have picked a more important and, in retrospect, disastrous period in German history. In the previous month Hitler had acquiesced in the murder of his old friend, the S.A. or *Sturm Abteilung* leader Ernst Roehm. Hindenburg the President had just died and Hitler had combined the offices of Chancellor and President. In fact his long speech on the occasion was relayed to the German boat on which Edith was travelling. Some time later Greta, who was the local leader of the *Bund Deutscher Maedel*, the female counterpart to the Hitler Youth, paid a return visit to England where her athletic form and blonde hair were much admired as she swam in the sea at Blackpool. My sister once had a curious conversation with Greta. Edith had been talking about my father's war service and suddenly said he might have killed one of Greta's fellow Germans. On the basis of pure wishful thinking Greta immediately said she was sure Mr Greenwood hadn't killed any Germans. My sister was shocked by the slogan *Juden Unerwunscht* 'Jews not wanted here' notices displayed in public places. There was one by the toilets in the restaurant on the Harz mountain.

Many years later this episode had an interesting sequel. On one of our many trips to Germany my wife Barbara and I paid a visit to the village where Edith had stayed. It still had old, cobbled streets and its remarkable twelfth-century church. We found some old people and I questioned them. They did not come from the region however, but from East Prussia, now no more. They had fled the advancing Russians, but, unfortunately for them not far enough, for the border of the West zone was still seven miles away.

As I mentioned earlier my sister had trained to become a secretary. This and her knowledge of German coupled with her intelligence and sense of responsibility enabled her to become not just a typist, but the private secretary to a German Jew who had founded a slipper factory in Blackburn, a mill town half way between Nelson and Preston. It produced Newman's slippers and the proprietor was called Jack Newman. When my brother Bobby was shot down and we still had faint hopes of his survival, my sister's knowledge of German was very useful in correspondence with the Swiss Red Cross. But sadly in the end his death was confirmed

Edith's kindly and responsible nature led her to become a member of a society which adopted lonely servicemen exiled from their countries because their countries had been occupied by the Germans. Edith had 'adopted' a most interesting Belgian from Charleroi called Roger Jacquemin.

He was a journalist, a profession I had the ambition to enter. Moreover I was in awe of him because he had actually had a book published. It was about Belgium, for he was an ardent patriot. Much to Edith's consternation he had a violent hatred of the Germans and said he could not wait to kill them. Edith was incapable of hating anyone. I suspect Roger brought the best chance of marriage Edith had ever had and indeed ever would have. But my mother disapproved vehemently of any such move. She had a violent dislike of the Belgians which did not help. After the war Roger married and he and his wife invited us over to their house in Charleroi. Charmingly they had named their little girl Edith. Sadly Roger died of a heart attack not long after.

There was one incident during a visit by Roger which made Edith cross, but which in retrospect I find amusing, even charming. It chanced that Roger, my half-brother Bobby, by then in the R.A.F., and my cousin Ralph then in the Merchant Navy, were all on leave in our house at the same time. Either Roger or Ralph threw out the challenge of a drinking competition so they all three went out on the town. I think Roger won. Bobby and Ralph were, as I recall, both sick.

Unfortunately, perhaps because of the privations and hardships of the war, Edith became very ill with glandular fever. This lasted a long time and affected her body and made her legs swell. This was around 1947 and 1948. At the same time my father started to become unwell. All this necessitated both my mother and sister giving up their well-paid jobs.

Because of her experience in the fur trade my mother decided to open a clothes shop in our local town Nelson. This need not have been disastrous save for two things. She persuaded my sister to go into business with her, partly so she could deal with the correspondence and 'do the books' as the saying is.

To compound this, my mother opened a second shop in the too quiet nearby Yorkshire town of Earby. This too was a failure. We had left our old terrace house on Holly Mount in Manchester Rd and now lived over the shop in very cramped conditions. I had to sleep in the same room as my father whose bronchitis was growing steadily worse. Another bad plan then entered my mother's head. She decided to build a large detached house in the poshest most expensive part of the town on a hill almost in the country. The builder went bankrupt and this involved us in debt. This compounded Edith's anxiety. She perhaps realized that in agreeing to enter into partnership with my mother she had destroyed her last chance of independence.

It was about this time that, around the age of fourteen, I enjoyed my first two holidays abroad, both to Cannes in the south of France, where glamorous yachts and glamorous people could already be seen, including Stewart Granger the handsome English film star of the time.

To put it unkindly he was a sort of cut-price Clark Gable, a fact which reflected the relative status of our two countries after the war. Near to Cannes in the mountain village of Vallauris adjacent to the sweet-scented perfumeries of Grasse, lived Picasso. We visited his pottery and bought two ceramic plates from his workshop, though we never actually met him or even saw him. We also saw and heard the famous and beautiful Juliette Greco sing. There was a third person with us. This was a sweet but not beautiful girl called Joan. Both she and her sister Tess were the daughters of a shopkeeper who had a shop not far from my mother's. Sadly and embarrassingly this led to a spell of bad blood between my mother and their father who thought my mother's shop was affecting his trade

Both Joan and Tess had served in the armed forces during the war. Here many a marriage was hatched. Tess had married a Polish exile. After the war, Joan, who was, like Edith a girl with a strong social conscience, worked on the continent assisting refugees and displaced persons. This is a delicate matter, but I suspect that Edith, sensing the doors of marriage closed to her, had developed Lesbian tendencies. I am not sure whether this entered her relationship with Joan, but I feel more certain that Edith developed a Lesbian attachment to a rather nice younger girl called Pamela. Pamela's father, as I recall, was a Delius fanatic and I often listened to records of the composer's work in his house. When and how Edith's relationship with Pamela ended I am not sure, about the time Edith went to Keele I think.

A final example of Edith's sense of responsibility and courage was her decision to stand post-war as a Conservative candidate in Nelson a factory town noted for the dominance of the Labour party. In fact the town had acquired the name of 'Little Moscow' during the Thirties. She was the only Conservative member of the town Council, but her powers of speech and her courage were such that, to adapt Macaulay 'Even the ranks of Labour could scarce forbear to cheer'.

7 MY BROTHER BOBBY

I have already mentioned my half brother was born Robert Winn in 1920 and that we always called him Bobby. He was therefore exactly twelve years older than I was, for I was born on December 23rd 1933, a fateful year in European history which saw Hitler's rise to power.

There is no love like that of an admiring younger brother for an elder one and of course to me Bobby was always a full brother, not a half one, just as Edith was always my full sister. In many ways I was a complete contrast with my brother, but this only made my admiration for his so different qualities the greater. I was bookish and impractical. He loved mechanical things such as his model railway. I can't remember whether he had any Meccano sets (they always baffled me), but I know he was a radio fanatic.

He built a radio set from spare parts complete with valves, whose function I never understood. I was heartbroken when I dropped it and it would not work afterwards. No wonder he became a wireless operator air-gunner in Bomber Command. Of course he knew all about cars, which are still mysteries to me, and was an excellent driver. He had a dog which he adored. He was devastated when it was run over by a train on the railway line just behind our house. I, on the contrary, have never been interested in having a dog.

As a timid boy going to a private primary school with cap and blazer I was a natural target for the local blazerless elementary school roughs. To use Lawrentian language I was a 'mardy arse'. So, when I started school before he had gone off to the R.A.F., he accompanied me as my guard. No one would have dared attack him. When he came home on leave I was so proud of his leather flying suit, his white silk gloves and his huge flying boots.

I remember so vividly the arrival of the news of his death. As usual I had gone to my father's club on the way home from school. We had taken the bus home from the town centre and were sitting in the kitchen having toast and tea. My father was reading the Blackburn paper *The Northern Evening Telegraph*. I think the headline was 'Cologne Bombed: Twenty-Eight Planes Missing'. Suddenly the doorbell rang. It was the dutiful telegraph boy with the fatal Air Ministry telegram with the words 'I regret to inform you' followed by the rank and name and the sad words 'Missing, believed killed'.

I think my father told me not to say anything till he came home from the cinema and could tell my mother himself, for he knew how devastated she would be. I felt sad, of course, but was also ashamed of the sense of self-importance I had at my being singled out from my friends by this bereavement.

8 SCHOOLDAYS

Because of my sister Edith's interest in literature I could read before I went to school. There was a primary fee-paying school that was part of a building which also contained a Methodist chapel up Railway Street not far from the town centre. I think my parents thought the free local elementary school might be too rough for me. Moreover both Edith and my brother Bobby had been to this school. It was run by a formidable spinster called Miss Washington who had also taught them. My brother Bobby used to escort me there in the early days to prevent any bullying by local roughs from the mill workers terraced houses.

I was five. I did not want to go to school. I wanted to stay at home with my beloved granny and Our Polish home help. As he was a cinema manager my father could be home for much of the day and so I wanted to be with him. Once settled in, however, I was quite happy at Miss Washington's. With her assistants she gave us a good basis in education. We even began elementary French with a textbook entitled *Le Livre Rouge*. We also had a young dancing teacher whose lovely legs aroused early sexual feelings. I also developed the usual infant crushes on one or two of the girl pupils. I was not very good at drawing and painting, but at this stage my mathematics, which consisted of elementary arithmetic, was satisfactory.

Later it was to become by far my weakest subject. Miss Washington used to take us on walks and point out the plants and flowers and teach us their names and characteristics. She also had a clever rhyming mnemonic which taught us the names of all the kings and queens of England from William the Conqueror onwards chronologically. This was a great asset for, as I have come to see, a correct chronology is the backbone of historical study. My later deep interest in history was aroused.

Nelson had no grammar school, and because all my family was at work and Bobby was away in the R.A.F. the problem of what to do about my schooling when I reached ten loomed. After my grandmother died I spent much time in the holidays with two spinsters who lived next door and who bore the good Lancashire name of Umpleby. Their first names were Sissy and Margaret. One day when I was about six I badly wanted a pee and they let me pee into a hot water bottle. The sight of my little penis afforded them the greatest amusement. Of course when she came home in the evening from work I confided this 'secret' to my mother and she was outraged with the sisters and for a time I was not allowed to go to their house.

At the back of the house was a cobbled street and beyond that the back gardens and then the railway cutting and the field beyond. This was a sloping field called the Hardplats with a wood to the right. On the long light evenings of double summer time I would play out there till late with any boys of my age who turned up. We usually played Cowboys and Indians and had toy pistols and rifles. We used to roll over in the long grass and pretend to be dead. This gave me sometimes a peculiar sensation in the summer heat. One day I met some rather threatening boys in a piece of woodland. I said that we ought to settle things in a reasonable manner and not by fighting, thus anticipating my later fascination with the great philosopher of peace, Thomas Hobbes. Another pastime after tea in the evening was to play street cricket with bat and tennis ball with two sisters, Betty and Pat from a house up the road. We also played table tennis indoors and I evinced an interest in Betty's legs when I bent to pick up the ball from the floor which amused both girls. I felt some pre-pubertal sexual stirrings for Betty, particularly as she had an interest in French and even possessed some French magazines.

My parents decided that I should go to boarding-school despite all my protests. Again they fell back on experience. They initially flirted with the idea of a public school and visited Sedbergh on the Yorkshire moors and even Eton which would surely have been beyond them financially.

Then they remembered that Ralph the son of my father's brother Ernest (he like my father had been in the First world War but at Gallipoli rather than in Flanders) had been a boarder at Kirkham Grammar School even though he lived in Blackpool and could have travelled the short distance to Kirkham as a day boy. Kirkham lies half way between Blackpool and Preston. It had once been a prosperous market town in the Middle Ages and had a ruined abbey whose prospect was to haunt my nightmares.

It also had a splendid parish church with a lofty spire. However it had fallen on evil times because the railway for some reason (perhaps the town did not want it) had passed it by. I sat an entrance examination there in English and arithmetic and passed even though I remember putting 'sheeps' as the plural of 'sheep'.

The school, which had a splendid long old building covered in Virginia creeper that turned the most wonderful red in autumn, had a distinguished history. It was founded in 1549 in the reign of Edward the Sixth for the study of grammar which, at that time, of course, meant Latin grammar since English as a barbarous

'Gothic' language was thought by many not to have a grammar worthy of the name. Thus did all our grammar schools get their name. Indeed no young person in this age of the computer can conceive what prestige the Latin language used to have. We were largely a Latin-based nation. Ben Jonson tells us that Shakespeare's Latin may have been small, but his Greek was even less. So in the grammar schools, if not in the public ones, Latin still took second place to Greek.

It was the mark of a gentleman to know Latin. A credit in O-level Latin was at that time a prerequisite for entering Oxford University.

The school had one house of boarders and I think six houses of dayboys from the Fylde area. Each house had about forty boys. The houses were named after the location from which the boys came: Fylde House. Blackpool House, Lytham House, Kirkham House, Preston House are the names I remember. The boarders' house was called School House. As the members lived at the school they could practice all sports at the weekends and always beat the others at rugby and cricket. School House always produced the *Victor Ludorum* as he was Latinately named or 'Victor of the Games' in the athletics competition in summer.

The eight or nine boys who entered with me in 1943 were boarded for their first term, not in the school dormitories, but in the house of the history master Mr Hughes and his kindly wife. She tucked us up every night and on Saturdays supervised our weekly bath. We would walk up to school for breakfast, as I remember, and school started at 9-0 with assembly in the impressive school hall. I was particularly impressed by a sabre on the wall which had belonged to an old boy from the school who had been an officer at the battle of Waterloo. Each new boarder was given an older boy as a mentor. School House had prefects who were allowed to administer corporal punishment with a slipper for minor misdemeanours. Every Sunday the whole house marched to town in a column of twos to attend the morning service. If I remember rightly during my first term the then headmaster the Reverend Cresswell Strange took the church service.

He had a reputation for administering a sound beating with the cane. One morning I had been sent out to stand in the corridor for inattention or for talking in class. I had heard that if the headmaster came down the corridor and saw someone sent out to stand there he would give the pupil a beating. The day I was sent out I heard him approaching and in my terror I wet my trousers. He walked straight past me and, in fact, I never had a beating from him.

Naturally, as someone in orders, he took the morning assembly which had a religious tinge with a pep talk and hymns. The noise in the hall before the masters entered was unbelievable. After two terms he was replaced by a much gentler man Dennis Norwood, who, I think had been a good scholar of Ancient Greek. I was to have an excellent relationship with him and he helped me to get into Hertford College Oxford at which his own son was a student.

At first I was deeply unhappy from homesickness. I cried a lot. After three weeks we could travel home after Saturday morning school for a break, but had to be back on Sunday night. Even though the distance was thirty-four miles or so I just had to go home by bus. I cried all weekend, begging not to be sent back. But there was no alternative. My father told me to be brave. Resignation was the only answer. Of course I adapted to school demands and routine, but I remember on cold autumn and winter days shivering as I stood in the tiled washroom and looked out of the windows to where the dismal R.A.F. camp stood behind barbed wire on the Blackpool bypass. It seemed a symbol of my own desolation. I was counting the days to the holidays and there always seemed such a lot of days to count. As always when one is longing for something, time just seemed to creep along. Counting the days seemed paradoxically to lengthen the waiting time rather than to shorten it.

As we boys matured sexually sex naturally had to find an outlet. When I was thirteen or fourteen an event occurred which brought this to a focus. I went with some of the other boys to a classroom with its old gnarled wooden desks on which generations of boys had carved their names. Here a boy with his flies open and his stiff penis protruding was masturbating and I was amazed to see a sticky white fluid appear.

Not long after that one of the leading athletes of the house who had a strongly muscular body happened to be alone with me and told me I had a rather feminine body. Then both of us rubbed against each others' thighs till ejaculation occurred. One prefect used to take boys into his bed after lights out despite the risk of discovery, as the housemaster's room was just outside.

Our first housemaster Mr Price was also a good music teacher and I learned to appreciate Beethoven and classical music from him. He also intimated to me that I could not sing in tune. With the piano teacher I never got beyond 'The Jolly Farmer'.

We had seen a handsome man in the splendid naval uniform of a lieutenant on a destroyer dining in with us on occasion. It turned out he was called Mr Crane and had been the housemaster when my cousin was a pupil in the thirties. When Mr Price left, Mr Crane returned as housemaster. He had served on Atlantic convoys during the war and had developed a great admiration for Americans and their 'know how'. He was amazed at the rapidity with which they could turn out ships. He was a keen and capable all-rounder at cricket. Many cricketers rather despise baseball as being a sort of rounders played with a hard ball, but he had been an enthusiastic spectator at baseball games. He was a strict disciplinarian and had a fearsome reputation for beating with a hard slipper boys who had misbehaved. I think there was one occasion on which he beat me, but only one.

Mr Crane played an important role in my life. He took a great personal interest in me. When I told him my parents had considered sending me to Sedbergh he said I would never have survived the cross country runs the boys had to take on the snow covered Yorkshire moors in the early winter mornings.

He was the gymnastics master and I was hopeless at gym. I could just about climb a rope but could not get over the vaulting horse or do hand stands like the other boys. But he was very indulgent. However I became a keen rugby player. Indeed I once scored a try by running the whole field after making an interception which a fellow pupil, who later played for his county, once told my father- in- law was one of the best tries he had ever seen.

Helped by Mr Crane's coaching I became a reasonably good batsman and opened for the school first eleven. I never had a big score. The highest score I got was in an evening knock about among School House pupils when I scored seventy runs. I used to watch Mr Crane play for the nearby village of Wrea Green.

He was a splendid batsman, bowler and fielder. I also liked going to the village because a rather pretty girl lived there and could be seen at the matches.

Smiling at each other with a word or two was as far as we got though. I think Mr Crane was aware of these 'goings on' to use an old expression.

He once asked us after evening 'prep' to write down a self-report on anything that was troubling us. I hinted at the problem of sexual thoughts and masturbation, saying I hoped to overcome the habit. He arranged for me to have a talk with the headmaster Mr Norwood.

Mr Norwood, who had a wife whose beauty we all admired, and who was also a very kind person, gave me a talk very much of the period in which he intimated the practice of pre-marital chastity made the delights of sex even more wonderful. It was because of Mr Norwood that I began to enjoy opera. He took a party of us to a performance of Bizet's Carmen by the Carle Rosa touring company in Blackpool. There could not have been a better initiation.

There was a notice board in the common room on which *The Daily Mail* was displayed each morning. I was told that from its early days it had acquired the nickname *The Daily Liar*. From 1943 to 1945 I scrutinised it eagerly for war news. Here I think what we now call 'spin' was imposed by the government to keep up morale. When I was at home my father and I also eagerly scrutinized the war news in what was then *The Daily Mail's* more successful rival, *The Daily Express*.

9 SOME SCHOOLMASTERS AT KIRKHAM GRAMMAR SCHOOL

I have already mentioned Mr Hughes as the master in whose house I boarded for my first term. He was to play an important part in my education for from the junior forms up to the sixth form he taught history. My interest in history was partly rooted in the mnemonic of the kings and queens of England learned by heart at Miss Washington's primary school.

It gave one a sense of chronology and chronology is central to the study of history. It was Mr Hughes's inspiring teaching, however, which confirmed history as my favourite subject. He was rather like the famous A J P Taylor in his ability to talk about a historical topic or period without a book or notes. He also had the ability to raise questions about the significance of historical events and about interconnections and parallels between them.

Keen to help prepare me for university he brought in a younger teacher called Mr Coates who had assisted him in teaching that crucial period the seventeenth century. Mr Coates coached me in the fraught political philosophy of that period. I shall always be eternally grateful to him for the small discussion group on the *Leviathan* of Thomas Hobbes which he held in the congenial surroundings of the excellent school library. This was to influence my teaching of that century as my special period when I became a lecturer, not in history, but in English literature in the 1960's at the University of Kent. I tried to interest students of literature in Hobbes because he is such an excellent writer.

Our English master Mr Williams was an admirable man. He had fought in the First World War. Unfortunately he was unable to keep order and so was mercilessly ragged in class. I am ashamed to say I joined in cheeking him. I am particularly ashamed because he was very kind to me and tried to encourage me in the study of literature. He gave me a copy of the poems of T S Eliot.

Our Latin master was Mr Middleton. He managed to instil enough Latin in me to enable me to pass prelims when I entered Oxford later. I also profited from his teaching of Roman history. I used greatly to enjoy reading Caesar's *Commentaries* on my own, but, alas, in English, so that it did nothing to improve my knowledge of the Latin language. I have sadly forgotten the name of my first maths teacher in the lower school where I hopelessly floundered in algebra. I have also forgotten the name of the older maths master who taught me in the upper school. I thought he was something of a dry stick and rather remote. He knew his subject thoroughly, but his teaching of geometry in particular was dry and uninspiring. He never used diagrams to explain the deductions and theorems of Euclid properly. It seemed that the thing to do was simply to learn the formulae by heart. But perhaps my lack of progress in the subject owed more to my incapacity rather than to his. It may be that I have forgotten the names of my maths teachers because of my own weakness in the subject. It has always been my worst, although a later interest in philosophy awoke an interest in the nature of mathematics and how it is related to other forms of knowledge.

As the physics and chemistry teachers were away at the war, I never learned those subjects so I did no lab work in them. However I was not entirely deprived of the study of natural science because we had an excellent biology teacher, a small dapper man called Mr Stevenson who also sometimes supervised sports and umpired at cricket. He taught us about osmosis and photosynthesis He told us about the Lysenko scandal. Lysenko was a Russian biologist who claimed, as Lamarck had done before him, that acquired characteristics could be inherited. He was approved of by Stalin who imprisoned his opponents. Mr Stevenson also gave me a piece of good exam advice. He liked my style in writing and emphasized the importance of a legible hand and good style in exams and how it pleased examiners. I think he half implied that a good written style might help to compensate for a certain deficiency in one's knowledge of the subject.

In the junior forms the languages Latin and French were taught by women. I can't recall the name of my Latin teacher, but remember her as rather beautiful and attractive. Our first French teacher was rather older and married to Mr Williams. She was formidable and intimidating and kept much better order in class than her husband could. The power to do this has always struck me as imponderably mysterious. It has nothing to do with physical force. As my son said of his experience at his school, it is a kind of aura. You just have it, or you don't. But when I reached the upper form for French, I had one of the best teachers of all Mr Lawton. He too was not very good at keeping order and we sometimes ragged him, but in a kindlier way than with Mr Williams.

Mr Lawton was deeply interested in literature. We read Racine's *Phedre* and Corneille's *Le Cid* with him. We used an excellent anthology *Nine French Poets* which had a particularly good selection of the French Romantics.

Mr Lawton had a great love for Baudelaire and I became fascinated by Baudelaire's poetry and his character as a *poete maudit*, an alienated figure, in some ways the first modern poet, as Eliot perhaps regarded him. I even wrote a sonnet in French imitating his sonnets which Mr Lawton gently corrected. I learned that key poem of symbolism 'Les Correspondances' by heart. This helped me a lot when I came to sit the Subsidiary level French exam when I recited it to the oral examiner who was very impressed. It was in Mr Lawton's class that I first heard the work of Jean Paul Sartre discussed. Mr Lawton was very keen on drama and decided on a school production of *Hamlet*. When I went to the rehearsals I had the somewhat vainglorious hope that I would be selected to play Hamlet, while at the same time being somewhat apprehensive at the amount of rote learning this would require.

Fortunately that amount fell quite within my scope for I was selected to play the part of what the ancient Greeks called a spear carrier, namely Marcellus who mainly figures only in the first act. However I still remember by heart his wonderfully poetic speech on how at Christ's birth the cock crowed all day long. On one evening I 'dried' as the saying goes. As I followed an exchange between Horatio and Hamlet, I became so absorbed in their exchange that I forgot to enter on cue. I had the indignity of being prompted and hoped the audience of parents didn't hear the prompt. I can't recall his name but the boy who played Hamlet was excellent.

A word about sport. As we practiced together at weekends we boarders had a great advantage when we competed against the other five houses in rugby, critic or athletics, and so we always won. Mr Crane was an excellent coach in every field of sport. In rugby I played wing forward. The task of each wing forward is to run round the scrum if the other side gets the ball and, without getting off-side, that is ahead of the ball, stop the other side's scrum half from passing to the three-quarters and starting an attack. My partner and I rushed round and crashed head on giving each other a bloody nose. Sometimes when we were practicing we played in a field where cows had grazed. I can assure you that playing rugby among the cow pats has its unsavoury side. I don't think Health and Safety would allow it today. When I was still quite junior I watched our house, which was called School House, defeat another house by one hundred points to nil

In rugby I never got above the house team, but in cricket I eventually got into the first eleven at the age of seventeen. Mr Crane had taught me an excellent batting style. I opened the batting and sometimes managed to stay in quite a while, but I never scored more than eight runs. I remember a particularly fraught match. I think it was away against Hutton Grammar School which had the reputation of having a fearsome fast bowler. I got one or two painful knocks. I think I stayed in a while but then was out to him LBW. I can still remember Mr Crane, who was umpiring, smiling at me as he raised his finger. At least I was out of the firing line. My top score was in an evening house practice knock about, not a serious game with another school. I got seventy runs.

Finally I must recur to Mr Norwood who became headmaster after the frightening Reverend Cresswell. Strangely enough though the Reverend Cresswell had been a beater, the school opening assembly in his time was like an unruly scrum even after the master's entered. Mr Norwood was not a beater and yet he soon had the school assembly open in dignified and respectful quiet.

He had a most beautiful wife. Once when he was surprised at a boy's complaining about being cold in bed at night he took it in good part when the boy cheeked him by saying: 'Yes but you have Mrs Norwood to keep you warm.'

He had a son who went up to Hertford College and was, I think, in his second or third year when I entered. Mr Norwood had been a good classical scholar and had been up to Hertford College Oxford. I think this greatly helped me to get a place as a 'commoner' as those who were not 'scholars' were called.

I elected to go to university before military service so I when I entered many of my friends there were two years older than I was having done their two years military service.

As I elected to go on to do post graduate work I went for my medical. I was found to have flat feet and, as compulsory military service was just being phased out I never had to do it. I thought this was very fortunate as I think I would have been very unhappy being 'bawled at by duffers' as H. G. Wells once unkindly put it. One young man I met in lodgings had had a friend killed in the Korean war. He had bent over a jammed trench mortar. It went off and the bomb decapitated him, so I might have escaped more than just square bashing.

I shall always be grateful to Mr Norwood. He was a kind and cultivated man who took a great personal interest in me. As I said earlier he encouraged my interest in classical music and opera as well as in learning.

10 FIRST LOVE

Oh gentle feelings, soft sounds, the goodness and greatness of a soul that has been moved; the melting happiness of the first tender, touching joys of love Where are you? Where are you?

This is the touching conclusion of Turgenev's novella *First Love*.
 I suppose I must have been about fifteen, so it would have been 1949, two years before I left school to go to Oxford University. I had already read with admiration and love the poetry of A. E. Housman and T. S. Eliot and started to write poetry myself. When I was at home I frequented Nelson's excellent local library near the town centre. It had been founded by Andrew Carnegie, as had many other libraries in industrial towns. It had an excellent selection of books on English literary criticism which included I. A. Richards's very influential *Principles of Literary Criticism*. There may have even been an early work on English poetry by my future tutor at Oxford F.W. Bateson. I think they later obtained a copy of his *English Poetry: A Critical Introduction* when it appeared in 1950, the year before I went up to the university. They may even have had some of the criticism of F. R. Leavis. Both these men were to become my spiritual mentors. Literature had long since been, as Carlyle had long ago said it was, the only living branch on the tree of religion.
 But, as well as the books, there was the lovely young library assistant, Mary. I soon noticed her bright

intelligent face and the prominent breasts under her immaculate white blouse. I began to pay her special attention, much to the flattering jealousy of one of the other girls who was not so attractive. She treated us with open sarcasm. As the library was Mary's workplace, we had to be careful. Soon, however, she agreed to meet me outside. On her afternoons off and in the long light summer evenings we would go for long walks in the surrounding countryside and woodlands which looked towards Pendle Hill, the famous 1800 foot high local whale- shaped local landmark.

As autumn drew on we would walk arm in arm along the river bank in the moonlight. We would kiss and embrace passionately under the trees, where, hidden from view, we would explore each others' bodies. Once I somewhat embarrassingly came to climax and ejaculated which made for an uncomfortable walk home.

In the dark winter evenings we would go ballroom dancing to the local dance hall, and even the dance hall in Burnley four miles away, where the popular band of Joe Loss used to play. They were often heard on the BBC at that time. Dancing in Burnley involved a four mile walk home late at night through the townlet of Brierfield between Burnley and Nelson. Then we would sit and kiss on the stone wall outside Mary's terraced house. Looming high directly next to the terrace was the gloomy weaving shed where Mary's father worked. His hearing had been impaired by the noise of the looms. He and Mary lived alone and loved each other dearly. I assumed he had been widowed. The family surname was Shackleton. Opposite the wall on which we sat and embraced so tenderly was a most unprepossessing and ugly shop which sold potted meat, much favoured at the time. However in our passionate kisses we were oblivious of the ugly and dreary nature of our surrounding. Love does not just conquer the world, it transforms the world.

Many years later I wrote a poem 'Her Father Loved Proust'. The first verse runs

*Her father worked in the mill
And loved Proust,
Pale blue volumes
Containing visions
Of a frieze of youth
I see him still.
His daughter
Stepped from the frieze
A vision,
An initiator into other worlds.*

The poem was printed on pages 52 and 53 of my privately published poetry collection Unfrozen Leaves.

On some days we went into the house, as when we played gramophone records. Her father was, of course, at work, so we had the place to ourselves. I used to gaze at her lovely photograph on a sideboard and, like Proust, wondered at what a whole life world of experience from a distinctive perspective lay behind those lovely features, a world not even our conversation could wholly bring to life. On one occasion we both stripped naked, but, in those days when contraceptives and contraceptive advice were hard to come by in a narrow small town environment dominated by puritan Nonconformists, there was a natural fear of pregnancy outside marriage. We were both too timid to proceed to full intercourse. Mary intimated that it was not yet the right moment for that venture. Discipline was the girl's task then, but I was far too timid to pose a real threat to her virginity

I missed Mary greatly when I was away at school, and, as I have said, eagerly awaited the small pink envelopes containing her love letters. I used to write sonnets to her and included one called 'April Love' in one of my letters. It was about our country walks together in the Spring. Alas, I kept no copy of the poem, much to my regret.

My mother, needless to say, totally disapproved of our affair, as mothers are apt to do. She is partially excused by her business worries and her having to attend my dying father.

Like her father Mary was very cultivated and well read. She greatly enlarged my somewhat narrow sensibility. She introduced me to the frivolous camp works of Ronald Firbank and greatly admired the Sitwells, whereas I was predestined to be a Leavisite and despise them as light weight. We discussed painters and went to art galleries together. She loved music. Her favourite piece was Delius's 'Walk To The Paradise Garden.' As we had had many such walks this piece was always associated with Mary in my mind. We also went to Sir John Barbirolli's Halle concerts in Manchester. This entailed a return late at night and more night walks of four miles back from Burnley bus station, where the Manchester bus stopped, to Nelson. If I recall correctly in some places the street lights went out at midnight. We both adored Tchaikovsky and Rachmaninov's second piano concerto. Mary named its plangently sweet slow movement 'the chocolate box' for its lovely tune.

To descend from these cultural heights, we often indulged in the practice then vulgarly called 'necking' which consisted of kissing and embracing in the double seats of the back row of the circle. As I was a cinema manager's son notice of this somehow got back to my mother who was not best pleased.

Our relationship continued into my first year at Oxford. She was very curious to know what my life there was like for, as most people at that time, she had a romantic Brideshead Revisited vision of Oxford long before the successful television series. Unlike myself she was steeped in the works of Dorothy L Sayers, another writer the Leavis's were to despise as middlebrow.

I found the atmosphere of Oxford life difficult to convey to her and the close of my first term was clouded by my father's death. His bronchitis had worsened and in the summer when I had read to him by his bedside in the nursing home he had mostly been asleep. Alas, we had grown estranged from our early close loving relationship. Though he was proud of my having got into Oxford and boasted of it to his friends, he had come to regard me as an intellectual snob. We had grown apart. Professor Murphy the Principal of Hertford, a Plato scholar, conveyed the news to me with great tact, intimating to me that my father's illness had taken a turn for the worse, when in fact he knew he was dead. So just before Christmas 1951 I was at home for his funeral.

But to return to the reasons for my growing estrangement from Mary. I have always been somewhat tormented by a strong libido and this affected me while I was a student. I used to wander the streets of Oxford (some of them in dubious quarters) in search of a prostitute to satisfy my lust. I never found any who paid any attention to me. They were naturally much more interested in the lucrative American servicemen who frequented the town from the base at Brize Norton. I even went and talked to prostitutes in Piccadilly. The going rate was £5. I remember an embarrassing encounter with a highly rouged girl in a shop doorway. I was uncertain whether we would have to do it there or go to some sordid room. But she sent me off with the proverbial flea in my ear and I slunk back to my lonely hotel room. None of the waitresses there took the least interest in my hopeful hungry looks.

I tactlessly confessed much of my torment to Mary and she was not sympathetic. We grew estranged and gradually our affair, which had given us both such delight came to an end. I later learned that she had married and gone to live in New York. Some years afterwards, when I was in that city I used to wander the streets wondering where she was and whether we might meet again. It was not to be. Cities are great swallowers of individuality.

I conclude by printing a Hardyesque poetic recollection of our love. It is on page 52 of Unfrozen Leaves:

Long Ago
Do you recall love's wakening might
So long ago?
The hawthorn hedges freshly white,
Mist rainbows in the shining light
So long ago?

All life was like an opening book
So long ago,
But now, I take a backward look
Along the path our story took.
Do you also?

Upon our love the sun has set
Long, long ago;
Yet it was such I cannot let
My so changed being quite forget
Its youthful glow.

Where are you now? What turn and twist
Since long ago
Has your life known? If you exist
Do you have memories that persist
From long ago?

11 AT OXFORD

My going up to Oxford in the Autumn of 1951 coincided with the sad end of my adolescent affair with Mary which I described earlier. In many ways this was a fraught time for me as I shall go on to show. Having read Dorothy Sayers's novel *Gaudy Night* (a gaudy is a college gathering when old students return for a celebration dinner), Mary was disappointed in the very little I could tell her. Certainly at that time I knew nothing about gaudies, though later I was to attend some. As I said earlier I was very disturbed by the problems of puberty at this time. I had even gone up to Soho which was notorious for streetwalkers, but had been too scared to approach them. I made the mistake of telling Mary about this and, if I remember correctly, she was not very sympathetic. Our affair was not consummated because at that time contraception was not easy to come by for shy young people and she was naturally afraid of becoming pregnant.

As I described earlier, my mother and sister had made the mistake of opening a small business which was unsuccessful. I had to sleep in the same room as my bronchial father. This was an attic above the kitchen and living room which were behind the shop. Shortly before I went up to Oxford (an achievement of which he was very proud even though he also felt estranged from me because he thought I had become an intellectual snob) he became so ill that he had to go into a nursing home. I did not realize that this was, in fact, a prelude to death. He spent most of the time during my visits sleeping, so I always took a book to read with me. I had the slight trauma of a car crash at the time. I was driving back from the nursing home when a woman stepped out without warning in front of the car. I had to swerve violently to avoid her and was hit head on by a bus which was fortunately going slowly, The car was badly damaged, but repairable. There were, of course, no seatbelts then but my seat was forced backward and so my head did not go forward into the windscreen.

Just before the end of my first term at Oxford my father died at the age of sixty-eight. The Principal of Hertford, a very kind scholar of Plato called Murphy, called me to his room. Out of kindness he told me that my father was very ill and so I needed to go home. He knew my father was, in fact, dead, but spared me the news till I was with my family. So I returned home for the sad funeral.

I have mentioned how much I think the recommendation of my headmaster Mr Norwood, who, I think had read classics at Hertford, had helped me to gain admission to the college. I had to sit two essay type examinations of three hours each and have an interview with the Principal. This sufficed to get me in. I had a much less happy experience in sitting for a scholarship at St Edmund Hall. Here there were six three hour papers over three days. One was a paper of Ancient Greek to translate which, to my shame, I had to leave blank as we had not studied Ancient Greek at school. Naturally I was failed.

At the time before starting to do English Literature and Language, as the school was then called because you could opt to continue with Anglo-Saxon, if you wanted to specialize on the language side, you had to pass what were called Prelims after two terms. This involved papers in Old English, which included passages from *Beowulf* to translate, a paper on tragedy which involved the study of Sophocles' *Oedipus Rex* in translation, *King Lear* and Aristotle's treatise on tragedy. We had lectures on the Aristotle. I was very grateful to this part of the course for it deepened my interest in the nature of tragedy, a subject on which I was later to write.

I was 'farmed out', as the expression was, for Old English to a Mr Horgan at New College just down the lane. He was a pleasant man, but, looking back on his teaching, I think it would have helped me greatly if he had taught me some phonetics. This would have greatly helped with the pronunciation of Old English. For literature we had a pleasant tutor who came into college to teach the three of us (for there were only three English literature entrants that year) who was working on a B.Litt. post graduate thesis on William Blake. His supervisor was F W Bateson of Corpus Christi College who was later to be my tutor. I already had some knowledge of F W Bateson because I had read his excellent *English Poetry: A Critical Introduction* which I had borrowed from the excellent local library where Mary worked. He was to be one of the greatest influences on my life.

My greatest trial was the Latin we had to do. We had to be prepared to translate passages from Book 4 and book 6 of Virgil's *Aeneid*. We were taught by a venerable scholar of Ancient Greek named Charles Hignett. I must have been the bane of his life because I think Greek was his great love. I can still remember his stentorian: 'Parse it Mr Greenwood' as, embarrassed and blushing and almost in tears, I struggle to guess at the to me opaque vocabulary.

I entered Hertford College as what was then called a 'commoner' rather than a 'scholar'. Scholars had won college scholarships through examinations. I had won a State scholarship, also through examinations, to cover my fees and expenses. Oxford was full of delightful, if quaint old customs, and commoners wore a short gown affectionately known as a 'bottom freezer' whereas scholars wore long gowns. These were supposed to be worn at all times and even though many of the students had been in the forces, undergraduates were forbidden to enter pubs and dance halls except for one called the Arlosh Hall.

The university had a sort of university police called 'proctors' and if you transgressed these rules they could be judge and jury as well and fine you. Each student was assigned a room with a small bedroom adjoining. A student also had a male servant or a 'scout' as he was then called. He kept the room clean and made the bed. I suspect many were ex servicemen for the Second World War. The scouts also ran a college bar in the basement each night after dinner where the beer was cheaper than in pubs. This was to be my embarrassing undoing on one occasion, as I shall recount. At that time, unlike today, there were no indoor latrines, though we had chamber pots. If we wanted to use a proper lavatory we had to cross the quadrangle through the freezing night to the unsavoury block of latrines behind the college chapel. This was also a point where you could climb over the wall into college if you were out after midnight when the gate was locked by the porter. One evening in my first term I just went on drinking and drinking. This led to unfortunate consequences for my chamber pot as well as my feeling queasy for a week. My scout shrugged it off and did not reproach me. Perhaps he felt I had learned my lesson.

In my first term I had a large room overlooking the famous Hertford College bridge an image of the Rialto in Venice I think, not, as is commonly supposed the Bridge of Sighs. But I am open to correction. It is now known to millions through the TV programme Lewis. I once walked over the top of it. I shared the room with a handsome student of medicine called John Flint. His mother ran a newsagents shop in Birmingham where he helped out when he was at home.

He was a boxer and an excellent rugby player. He became a doctor, but eventually gave it up to farm cattle in the West country. I met him once in Oxford and introduced him to my younger son Edward who was reading French at Wadham College. Sadly John died four years ago. I sometimes also played rugby for the college team along with John, but oddly never cricket, my favourite sport, though I would watch the university team play county, and sometimes even test, sides in the university parks in North Oxford.

I loved college life. Alas I often slept in and so was too late for breakfast. But I used to love college dinners where we had the ritual of standing up when the Principal and fellows came past to sit on high table at the far end of the room. We had the quaint custom of sconcing. A fellow undergraduate could appeal to the head of your table that you be sconced if you had violated some minor point of etiquette. This meant you were brought a four pint silver goblet of ale and had to try to drink it all in one go. If you did not succeed, the goblet was passed round the table.

But what really both delighted and moved me was the sense of history sitting there in hall and seeing the splendid portraits of former members of the college looking down on you as though it was yesterday. So many Oxford colleges have strong links with my favourite period the seventeenth century, St John's with the luckless and tragic Archbishop Laud, for example, and Oriel where King Charles the First held court during the Civil War. I used to look up in amazement at the University Chancellor Clarendon of the Clarendon building where the Oxford University Press was housed on the basis of his six volume *History of the Great Rebellion*, a work I was later to read in its entirety when I was a graduate student His portrait was directly next to that of my beloved Thomas Hobbes. They were both from Wiltshire and friends. But Clarendon took umbrage at Hobbes's making his peace with the Cromwell regime with his *Leviathan* and wrote a book denouncing his 'pernicious errors to church and state'.

Here was I, a shy twentieth century student, directly connected to a living past. I loved the college quadrangles with their quiet shaded walks. I developed a particular love for the quintessentially Oxfordian Matthew Arnold. I was later to be awarded the then princely sum of thirty-five pounds for the Matthew Arnold Memorial Prize Essay. The title of my thirty-thousand-word essay was 'The Oxford Sentiment in the Work of Matthew Arnold'. Thirty pounds was a considerable sum in the 1950s. I suppose it would be worth around £200 today. I spent it on books in Blackwells including some by him. Like him, I too regarded the beautiful city of Oxford as 'the home of lost causes and impossible loyalties.' I particularly liked his essay 'Falkland' in his lesser-known collection *Mixed Essays*.

Arnold deprecated the title saying it reminded him of mixed biscuits. Lucius Cary Viscount Falkland was a friend of both Clarendon (who wrote a wonderful account of his life and his death at the battle of Newbury) and Hobbes and many other famous men of the time. He had a country house at Great Tew twenty or so miles north of Oxford where these friends met.

Clarendon called Great Tew (now unfortunately demolished) 'a university in little'. The friends who met there included Chillingworth who wrote on theology, Selden a clever lawyer who confounded the anti-royalists in parliament with his wit, and the poet Cowley. Cowley later left an unfinished poem on the civil war in which he wrote a sad account of Falkland's death at the battle of Newbury. I was to name my first son Matthew Falkland Greenwood after him. It was reading Matthew Arnold's essay on Falkland which stimulated me to read Clarendon. Both Thucydides and Clarendon write in notoriously difficult styles, Clarendon in long neo-Ciceronian periodic sentences. Hobbes, who had also been a member of Falkland's Great Tew circle, often writes in short laconic sentences as when he says of his friend Sidney Godolphin in the review and conclusion of *Leviathan* that he was slain 'by an undiscerned and undiscerning hand'.

I passed prelims. I often wonder if they were tender to my Latin because they knew of my keenness on English literature. Perhaps even the curmudgeonly Hignett relented. We used to have a meeting with the Principal and fellows at the end of each term in which we were told if our work had been satisfactory. I think it was called 'responsions' but am not certain and looking back I think it was held after we had started on part two in the Trinity or summer term. As I said earlier I was sent to F. W.Bateson at Corpus Christi college as Hertford at that time had no English teachers, but three classics ones. I suspect that the proportion is now reversed. At first all three of us, a Londoner called Colin and a boy from the Northeast whose surname was Hetherington and myself had a joint tutorial, but this then dropped in the second year to two and finally I had the privilege of a single tutorial. These single tutorials were one of the greatest pleasures of my life. Freddy Bateson as his colleagues called him was a shy retiring man originally, I think, from Cheshire. He lived in Brill in Buckinghamshire and his wife brought him in by car each day. He had been connected with the Ministry of Agriculture in the Second World War. He was a socialist and had written a pamphlet on agriculture from a socialist viewpoint. His great love was poetry about which he was extremely knowledgeable and an excellent teacher of the power to appreciate it. I could not have been luckier in the time at which I became his pupil for, an admirer of the Cambridge critic, F. R. Leavis's critical periodical Scrutiny, he had just founded the journal *Essays in Criticism*. Leavis used to come to Oxford to give lectures at the Literary Society and the two sometimes had interesting exchanges. Bateson admire the critical powers of Leavis, but sometimes felt his scholarship was faulty. Leavis had no qualms about making it clear in the exchanges that he resented this.

12 AT OXFORD PART TWO

The room in Corpus where I had my tutorials with Bateson was a most pleasant one. It was large with comfortable seats. We sat opposite each other. The room was very light because it had a window behind my tutor which looked out on the inner quad and a window behind me which looked out on the footpath between Merton Street and Christ Church meadow. Merton college with its square tower and ancient chapel was just across the way. The tutorial lasted an hour. I didn't want it to come to an end, but the lovely chimes of Merton's clock marked each quarter.

Bateson thought the time for reading English literature from Chaucer to Wordsworth, where at that time the syllabus ended, was too short, and so rather resented the amount students had to spend on *Beowulf* in the early stages. After all Chaucer himself would not have been able to read *Beowulf*. The method was for Bateson to assign the week's reading. In the case of Chaucer it might be some of the short poems such as 'The House of Fame' in the second week the Prologue to *The Canterbury Tales* and a couple of the tales. The third week might be more tales. Then in the fourth week *Troilus and Criseyde* and some of the minor poems with possibly some more tidying up. Bateson was a great lover of Chaucer. It was at this time that he brought out his book on Wordsworth with its acute remarks on Wordsworth's style in the *Lyrical Ballads* and its speculations about the psychology of the poet.

We looked at some Lydgate and then passed on from the somewhat dreary fifteenth century to the delights of Sir Thomas Wyatt the famous Kentish man and diplomat in the time of Henry the eighth. It is thought that he was one of Anne Boleyn's lovers before she married Henry the Eighth. She probably inspired the lovely poem that begins 'They flee from me that sometime did me seek'. Wyatt introduced the Petrarchan sonnet into English and one of his most haunting sonnets is the one which begins 'Whoso seeks to hunt I know where is an hind' is also thought to be about his fraught relationship with Anne. It refers at the end to her being 'Caesar's', that is the King's. Wyatt was imprisoned for a time in the tower of London and he wrote a striking poem about being made to witness the execution of Anne Boleyn's lovers from his cell window. We then moved on to the eloquent but less exciting Earl of Surrey who also wrote sonnets.

This brought us to the Elizabethan golden age and Sir Philip Sidney, the soldier poet who composed the sonnet sequence *Astrophel and Stella*, and to Shakespeare.

Bateson was not a very well man. Many years later I was at an English conference at which he collapsed foaming at the mouth with what I presumed was an epileptic fit. When we moved on to the metaphysical poets of the early seventeenth century and to the poetry of Ben Jonson he became ill for a while so I had to go to another teacher. Here again I was incredibly privileged for the teacher chosen was J.B Leishman at St John's college. I had already heard him lecture on Wordsworth. He was writing a book on Andrew Marvell and took me for single tutorials on that poet whose 'Ode on Cromwell' gives such insights into the politics of the period from a somewhat Hobbesian standpoint. It has always been one of my favourite poems as have his pastoral 'garden' poems. For some reason Leishman was not too well treated by the college and did not have a room where he could teach there. This is one of those strange anomalies of Oxford for he was world famous for his translations of the German poet Rilke. He had a college flat in Bardwell road in North Oxford. He held his classes there in a room completely lined with books, including, if I recall aright, a complete set of the works of D. H. Lawrence. At one end of the room was a music stand. It was standing there I understood that he did his translation work. He had also produced a parallel text of thirty odes by Horace.

Like Mallarme before him he had his 'Thursdays'. Every evening around eight a select band of pupils would assemble in his flat for coffee and conversation. He was particularly fond of playing records of Beethoven's mystical late quartets. Through this and reading J. W. N. Sullivan's book on the composer, I developed a great fondness for the movement in Opus 132 called the 'Heiliger Dankgesang' the holy song of thanks for recovery from an illness.

Bateson regarded him as a friend, but once remarked with regret that Leishman 'had become a crusty old Tory'. I had never noticed anything political in Leishman's talk and thought the remark spoke more to Bateson's views that to Leishman's. Sadly Leishman later died of a fall in the Swiss alps while out hiking.

Bateson recovered in time for me to read Milton's 'Lycidas' and *Paradise Lost* with him. We then moved on to the Restoration period and the vigour of Dryden's satires in defence of King Charles the Second against the Republican Earl of Shaftesbury. After Dryden we spent a long time on the elegant Pope some of whose poems, notably the *Moral Epistles*, Bateson edited. He also edited a comprehensive edition of Pope published in the excellent series Longman's English Poets. It was most enjoyable and inspiring to read this great poet along with Dr Johnson's splendid life of him. Bateson was most amused when I referred to Pope's 'Anglicanism' for, as he informed me, Pope was a Roman Catholic and suffered the disabilities imposed by those intolerant times. I still ruefully think that what comes through in his work is Poe's Toryism rather than his Catholicism and, of course, Toryism then went with Anglicanism. Only from the rococo-gothic romance *Eloisa and Abelard* with its touching portrayal of Eloisa's cloistered devotions might one suspect roman Catholicism in the author.

Now came splendid sessions on Blake, who was one of Bateson's favourite poets, more particularly for his compressed and vatic lyrics rather than the wordy and obscure *Prophetic Books*. Bateson was particularly interested in the way the accompanying engravings by the author could aid in interpreting his antinomian symbolism. Blake's antinomianism, his revolt against the sexual repressiveness of Christianity, in some ways anticipates Nietzsche. I think Bateson admired both but when I once asked him about Nietzsche on Christianity he replied that Christianity was not a unity but had taken several forms. Having studied Nietzsche intensively since I think Nietzsche recognized that multiplicity. It is interesting that in his splendid, if too short, essay '*Literature and Atheism*' in *Essays in Critical Dissent* Longman 1972, Bateson, favourably invoked Shelley's splendid pamphlet of 1811, '*The Necessity of Atheism*'. This pamphlet got Shelley sent down from Oxford, an act for which his epicene naked statue in University college chapel, of all places, does not atone. Bateson goes on to say that a crucial issue in our culture is 'the individual's attitude' to death. Earlier in the essay he had said that we are now 'compelled to objectify our ethical ideals in some non-religious mode'. Leavis is invoked in Bateson's affirming that 'literary instruction takes the place of religious instruction'. Surely Nietzsche stands behind this, though he is not mentioned. He is referred to somewhat cautiously in Leavis's fine essay on tragedy in *The Common Pursuit*.

We were now nearing the end of this marvellous course. We had reached the great Romantic poets: Wordsworth, Coleridge, Shelley, Keats and Byron. Of these it was Wordsworth and Keats who get most attention from Bateson. We read his thoughtful letters as well as his poems. We also read the fine essays of his friend and admirer Hazlitt along with the strange and sad *Liber Amoris*

Hazlitt's account of an unhappy love affair. We both warmed to Hazlitt's 'gusto' and his radicalism. I agreed with Bateson in his total distrust of the later Eliot's adoption of stilted Anglican attitudes and his criticism of Eliot's much touted and overhyped view of a mysterious 'dissociation of sensibility' in the seventeenth century, a piece of empty phrase making taken out of its quite different context in an essay by the French symbolist critic Remy de Gourmont. Bateson helped to put an end to the extraordinary vogue Eliot's essay had had.

And so came the ordeal of finals four days of three-hour exams, one in the morning, the other in the afternoon. At that time graduate work did not have in Oxford the aura it possessed in America. Bateson was instrumental in promoting a two-year 50,000-word essay for a B.Litt. as preferable for some students to the more 'scholarly' training in editing some ponderous largely unread past work for the twice as long PhD. The difference was that this did not give you the title of doctor which was required for university teaching in America.

It soon became clear, however, that the Oxford B.Litt. was highly regarded in America and I was later to teach there, first in Buffalo for a six-week summer school and then at the University of Santa Barbara near the lovely town with its old mission. Bateson hoped I was going to get a first. I can't be sure now, but I think I had a viva, but came away with an upper second. However, this turned out to be enough to enable me to do a further two years financed study with the view to my proposed thesis 'Matthew Arnold's Literary Criticism.' While still as student I had attempted to write a novel on my early years and my affair with Mary and my sexual torments. I have lost the manuscript but I recall a rather lurid description of the erotic atmosphere of a dance hall such as Mary and I had attended. Bateson kindly looked at the manuscript and kindly flattered me by saying I had the unteachable narrative gift'. He advised me to try to learn from reading Joyce's *Portrait Of The Artist As A Young Man* a work I came greatly to admire. It was about this time that Amis's *Lucky Jim* came out. Yes, we all envied him. The poems of Philip Larkin had started to appear, and Bateson was full of praise for them in his review. Bateson preferred the genre of poetry to the genre of the novel though, of course, he admired some novels. He later wrote an article about the novel's 'original sin'. This turned out to be filling out the story by lots of description of surrounding trivia, the curtains or furniture for instance. This he claimed was partly to work the confidence trick that if you remembered such small things the story must really have happened and not be merely a made-up fiction. I had been writing poems since I was fourteen, but I never showed any of them to him at this time because I did not think they were good enough.

I never managed to get any of them in either of the student magazines *The Isis* and *The Cherwell*. I had some poet friends who did, notably George MacBeth who was later to work as a BBC producer in Glasgow. My one successful piece of 'networking' was his getting a talk by me on the radio when I was working at the University of Glasgow.

I now come to the pivotal event of my life my meeting my future wife Barbara. This must have been in the summer term of my second year, 1952. There were, of course, very few women students at Oxford then and I never met anyone with whom I 'clicked' as the vulgarism has it. So I went to dance halls, the permitted one, Arlosh Hall which therefore was frequented by many students, and the one in the High street which was forbidden to students, but well attended, particularly by shop girls and nurses from the Radcliffe Hospital then just off the Banbury road where the Observatory now stands. The story of our meeting is not so much Dante and Beatrice, or Petrarch and Laura, as rather the Hollywood 'eyes across a crowded room' of the then popular song. I noticed this beautiful face and fine figure in a white blouse sitting opposite and went to ask her for a dance. We had only had one dance when I asked her if she would like to go for a drink. She agreed at once. We walked up the High street to The Golden Cross in the Cornmarket.

This was the historic hostelry where Shakespeare had stayed when he was journeying between Stratford and London. Alas it has now disappeared. We got talking over drinks and found out about each other's background and families. We seemed very compatible. She was an intelligent girl who had done well in school certificate, but, as I have said earlier, not many girls went on to university in those days. She had, however, gone on to teacher training college after a brief spell working in a bank for she was good at arithmetic, much better than I was. She was teaching at a small church school at Cassington a small village out on the road to Cheltenham. She told me amusing stories about the village children, mostly the offspring of agricultural labourers. One was about a boy called Gerald and was very amusing. She had been reading aloud the story of the Resurrection as was natural in a church school. When she said 'and he rose from the dead' Gerald blurted out 'that ad' the buggers'.

I then walked her back to her lodgings in Park Town. This was in a beautiful house in Regency terrace style which was rented by her landlady and her landlady's husband. The landlady provided breakfast and evening meals as was quite common in Oxford in those days. That house would now cost over a million pounds. We never knew what her husband did other than be about the house. They were spiritualists and in the evenings we were very amused by the strange moanings and groanings which emanated from the kitchen as the landlady tried to contact those who had 'passed on' to the 'great beyond'.

13 AT OXFORD, PART THREE

In a memoir one often reflects on what might have been. I read English Literature instead of history, the subject in which I had got my best marks. Since reading the populariser Joad, who gave me a knowledge of Socrates and Plato, and some selections from Aquinas at the age of fourteen, I had had an interest in philosophy. I even remember entering into philosophical discussion about Socrates with a man who was addressing a small crowd on Blackpool promenade (a somewhat downmarket replacement of Athens). Now Oxford was positively crawling with philosophers when I was there. It was said that there were more philosophers to the square mile in Oxford than anywhere in the world

There was a galaxy of brilliant thinkers there: Anscombe, Austen, Berlin, Foot, Hampshire, Hare, Murdoch, Ryle, Strawson and others. I could have attended their lectures, for lectures in all humanities subjects were open to all humanities students, but I did not go to a single philosophy lecture. Of course this was largely because I was absorbed in preparatory reading for my weekly essay for F W Bateson. The procedure was that he would make comments on the essay and then take it in to return it with a mark and further written comments.

This is not to say that I could not have found time to spare for I wasted the mornings far too often. To begin with I would sleep in and miss breakfast. Then instead of going to an eleven o'clock lecture, as I could have done, I went off for coffee and cakes in the Kemp café. This was above a shop located near where Broad street joins the Cornmarket. Now a singular reflection. I suspect the American philosophy, politics and psychology student Frank Cioffi was in there when I was. He would have been holding forth to his friends who might have even included Rupert Murdock. Later he would be colleague of mine at the newly founded University of Kent. Whenever a new college opened he would move to it, starting with Rutherford and then moving to Eliot. He then started the philosophy department at the newly opened University of Essex. He was a careful expositor of Wittgenstein and later became world famous for his criticism of Freud, his lecture on the BBC 'Was Freud a liar?' (he was) creating quite a scandal. I often reflect on what difference to my life it would have made if I had got to know him then. He once told me an amusing story about Iris Murdoch. He had asked her whether if she were the only girl in the world and he were the only boy she would go to bed with him. Here witty reply was that if he were the only boy in the world and she the only girl, she would consider it.

In a memoir one can also be confused and vague about chronology unless one has kept a diary which I did not. Diaries require discipline and time. I have already mentioned I cannot quite locate in time the occasion on which I first met Barbara at a dance, but I recall salient periods of what might be called the beginning of a long courtship. I call it that because though I found her very attractive and that we much enjoyed making love, we did not consummate our courtship till after our marriage in July 1958. I had lived in various lodgings as a graduate student and with the help of finance from my mother, particularly when my grant ran out.

I rented the attic flat at number two Church Walk near Summertown. This was very close to Park Town where Barbara lived and to the park of North Oxford where we would take delightful summer evening walks. That building now houses a distinguished centre for European studies. At the time there was a doctor Swithinbank from the Radcliffe on the second floor and a Swiss family on the ground floor.

My flat had no bathroom, so Dr Swithinbank kindly let me use the one on the second floor. He was very cheerful and kindly and, indeed, helpful. Once when a cyst rose on my wrist he cured it with an injection. He also treated me if I had a cold. Barbara and I sometimes entertained together some of my student friends. I remember a very genial evening with Stuart Hall who came from Jamaica. He later joined Richard Hoggart in founding the famous Centre For Cultural Studies at the University of Birmingham. I think I met him along with Mark Kinkead-Weekes, who was later instrumental in getting me to the University of Kent as a colleague when the university had just opened and was recruiting. I was teaching English literature at the University of Glasgow at the time and I met him again when he came to give a lecture on Kipling. In fact there was quite a flight from the so-called Celtic fringe universities to the new ones in England at the time. I think I met Stuart, Mark and another student named Tom Coulson at a lecture by C.S. Lewis.

Lewis was a spellbinding lecturer, unlike the boring Tolkien whose lectures I seem to remember as simply listing the etymologies of words in *Sir Gawain and the Green Knight* without bringing out the literary qualities of the work at all. It was not as hard as *Beowulf* had been. Its anonymous author was a contemporary of Chaucer's but wrote in a Northern dialect perhaps Cheshire or even Lancashire as the phrase 'nobbut an old cave' (the dwelling of the Green Knight) indicates. Chaucer is much easier to understand because it was his dialect which mutated into modern English. Lewis stood before us without a note and said we should treasure him because he was the last remaining medieval man. This was I thought hubristic but oddly compelling. He' knew his onions' as they say.

Barbara had a close friend, Sheila, who was also a teacher and rather jealous of Barbara simply because Barbara had a relationship, and she didn't. Late she married a charming Scotsman and settled down in Ayrshire, Burns territory, and had a family. After Barbara and I had moved to Canterbury they came down to see us and we passed a very pleasant occasion. I have already mentioned that Barbara was teaching at the village school in Cassington and that she had to bicycle there. I was particularly worried about her having to do this, especially on dark winter mornings and evenings for, of course, she had to start the ride about 7.30 in the morning. In winter ice was, of course, it was dangerous. A bigger new school opened at Kidlington which is nearer but still involved biking a few miles on a busy road. I myself had never learned to bike and it was, in fact, Barbara who taught me. I learned to ride around Park Town off the main road.

My study of Arnold proceeded well. We had a set of lectures under the rubric 'Sources, Methods and Authorities' given by the Coleridge and Hopkins scholar Humphry House. He was an excellent lecturer, initiating us into the byways of Victorian literature. In particular he insisted on the importance of the periodicals produced for family reading by the educated middle class which were such a feature of the time, weeklies like the *Saturday Review* where Leslie

Stephen's brother Fitzjames played a big role and Bagehot's *The Economist*. There was also *The Spectator*. George Eliot contributed to the *Westminster Review*. Dickens, of course, had had his own periodical *Household Words* and there was *Macmillan's Magazine* in which much of Arnold's work appeared. All the periodicals I needed could be consulted in the splendid Bodleian Library, where I took copious notes on them.

My supervisor for the thesis was John Bryson of Balliol College, the same college that Arnold attended. He was a member of a family engaged in shipbuilding in Belfast and very wealthy, rumoured to be a millionaire if I remember rightly. I think his own scholarly publication was rather exiguous, confined to an introduction to the excellent Reynard library selection from Arnold's prose and poetry which he had made. Arnold was born in 1822, that is twenty two years before Nietzsche. He died in 1888, the year T S Eliot was born. He was the son of the famous reformer of public schools Dr Thomas Arnold the headmaster of Rugby School and a classicist who put a high value on a classical education. Both Arnold and Nietzsche were Hellenists but neither was aware of the other's work. Both wrote of Emerson, but Arnold was more critical of him than Nietzsche. Both thought little of Carlyle whom Arnold called 'a moral desperado'. Both were deeply interested in, and knowledgeable about, religion and about Christianity in particular. The great difference was that Arnold wished to preserve Christian morality without belief in Christianity while Nietzsche wished to get rid of both.

My having studied up to French Subsidiary level with Mr Lawton was a great help to me in my study of Arnold, for Arnold, like Nietzsche was a great admirer of French writers. He overrated Sainte Beuve. He greatly admired too the Renan Nietzsche abominated. He was interested in, but critical of Flaubert, as was Nietzsche. So I read widely in the French writers Arnold admired. I also read excellent later French critics such as Paul Bourget, Remy de Gourmont and the religiously tormented Jacques Riviere, the editor of the *Nouvelle Revue Francaise* and the friend of Andre Gide. My father's pride in my getting into Oxford had led him to buy me life membership of the Oxford Union. I made much use of the splendid library there. The library had a complete set of Remy de Gourmont's *Promenades Litteraires*. My fifty thousand word thesis progressed well. It was while writing it that I wrote my three-thousand-word essay on the oxford sentiment in Matthew Arnold for the Matthew Arnold Memorial prize which I was awarded. It was my supervisor John Bryson who had read it and he told me he recognized my distinctive style. He took me out to dinner and then back to his flat in Belsize Court off Banbury road. I was deeply impressed by the fact that he had original drawings of ballet dancers by Degas on his walls. His telephone went and he answered with familiarity 'Hello David.' I realized he was talking to Lord David Cecil. I knew Leavis despised Cecil's work as too 'belle-lettristic', but I quite enjoyed the lectures on the nineteenth century novel which he delivered in his somewhat affected voice.

Barbara was very interested in my work on Arnold. Later on she was herself to study literature at university level. Her parents Douglas and Ella Watts lived in Slough in a semi-detached house in Bower Way off the Bath Road. They both came from Tredegar in South Wales, the home town of Aneurin Bevan the famous labour politician whom Barbara's father greatly admired. His statue stood just outside the town.

Barbara's father had been a coalminer, but like many miners had been laid off in the 1930's. It was at this time a trading estate on the Bath Rd in Slough was opened in which there were several light industries. Again, like many they went to Slough where houses were going up with affordable rents. They could never afford to buy their house. My m other already had the typical suspicion of a mother for her son's choice and their labour politics was also a bad mark in her eyes. They had a son Dennis who was rather pale and plump but not unathletic for he had a great love of fencing. He had done very well at school like his sister Barbara, but, again, like most at the time he had gone straight into work. He had the responsible job of Magistrate's clerk, the advice to the lay magistrates on points of law. He was studying at night school to get further law qualifications which he eventually did. This brought promotion to chief clerk. But he had to move to Kendal near the Lake district to take up his post. Sadly he had a weak heart, and perhaps under the strain of it all he had a severe heart attack, and died immediately. I should have mentioned perhaps an even stronger reason for the strain. He had married a young girl, Margaret Watts, who after having had two children died of cancer at the age of thirty.

Her parents were the dreariest souls, quite unlike Barbara's vivacious parents. But by some miracle they had produced a beautiful girl. She was only about thirty-five when he died. She had a wonderful soprano voice, but no real knowledge of the Mozart whose arias she could sing. After her untimely death Barbara's mother had to look after the children, but fortunately the elder, Gregory, was adopted by a childless couple she had got to know at the chapel she attended. This eventually was to give rise much later to a most painful episode in our lives when Barbara and I were married which I shall recount at the proper time.

My work on the thesis proceeded well. I found a typist who was familiar with academic conventions, as were many typists in Oxford at the time before word processers, and the bound thesis looked very presentable. Then came the viva or oral examination. One of my examiners was J. I. M. Stewart who had just produced the volume on the twentieth century which conclude the Oxford series of histories of English literature. It was unusual in that it abandoned the usual historical format and consisted of eight critical essays on eight major twentieth century authors. Both examiners were genial and put me at my ease at once intimating that the degree would be awarded. What then?

Naturally I had academic ambitions, but I had not yet had any articles published. I did not get anything into *Essays in Criticism* until the article on the style of George Herbert's sonnet 'Prayer' in January 1965. The next stage was to try for a research fellowship. In the meanwhile I was, in effect sponging on my mother and sister as I continued living in the flat in Oxford. Mr Bryson got me a little pin money for cleaning the dust off sixteenth century books in St John's library. I remember there were some horrid woodcuts of torture during the religious persecutions of that age in them. Human beings' inhuman cruelty never ceases to amaze me. Eventually I was invited to an interview for a fellowship at the prestigious and beautiful Magdalen College which possessed a famous deer park. It was a fearsome affair with all the fellows present.

Some of them seemed visibly irritated as I attempted to answer the points put to me, presumably about future research projects. It seemed that none of them was viable. I could not have performed too badly though, for afterwards one of the fellows who was an expert on medieval literature and who came from New Zealand wrote me a kind letter in which he said he was sorry that I had not been successful, but adding that if I ever applied for an academic post in the future I could name him as a referee. Of course university posts in English were few and far between as there were so many English postgraduates there was fierce competition for them. The new universities did not come until the sixties except for Keele. There were three things I did not know then. First that some New Zealanders had an extraordinary interest in Old and Middle English, in one case I met, even in Old Norse. Second that because my referee was a well known New Zealander his recommendation was of great help in getting me my first academic post which was at Christchurch in New Zealand, and third that quite fortuitously the University of Keele was to play a great part in my life and save me from despair at my own sense of uselessness which at times made me feel suicidal.

    I decided to take an exam for entry into the civil service. It consisted of two three hour essay type papers. I did not know what branch I was destined for as the exam did not state this. Consequently I had some hopes I would get an interesting post in the diplomatic core and be sent abroad. Eventually I was informed that I had been appointed a factory inspector and was to start work in the near future in the pottery town of Stoke on Trent. As I hardly knew a drill from a lathe this was certainly going to be a classic case of the square peg in a round hole. I am about to recount one of the most unhappy and fraught periods of my life in which I would walk the streets of that then smoky and dismal town and feel it would be better if I ended my life. I was to be saved by Barbara's joining me after our marriage. The marriage certificate for July 29th 1958 gives my occupation as factory inspector.

14 IN THE FACTORY INSPECTORATE

The terrible conditions in factories during the industrial revolution with the child labour and long hours forced even Tory governments such as that of Sir Robert Peele (who was himself a manufacturer) to health and safety legislation. But legislation needs to be enforced and so the Factory Inspectorate was created. Many women made their careers in it.

When I entered the Stoke office to 'learn on the job' after a short period of instruction, the Chief Inspector was a kindly, but formidable woman. She oversaw some of my first reports on factory visits. An inspector had to have learned the Factory Acts. At least once every year every major factory down to the small workshop, garage and scaffold site had to be visited. This involved a lot of legwork. The visits were primarily advisory, but if gross violations of the act (which also covered working hours and conditions as well as the guarding of dangerous machinery) were discovered the firm could be taken to court and, if found guilty, fined. In the most extreme cases imprisonment could follow. In the case of scaffolding, the scaffold must, of course, be secure so it would not collapse.

Toe boards, as they were called, must be present to avoid tools falling from the scaffold and injuring passersby. In factories proper clothing had to be worn so no one was trapped in machinery. The most difficult thing was the vertical drill. This had to be guarded so a worker's fingers were not trapped or, in the case of women, hair was not caught. However a guard often impeded the worker's vision, so guards were sometimes removed by the workers themselves. The law had however imposed what is called 'strict liability'. The guarding of drills was a duty for which the employer was completely responsible. It was up to the employer to see their employee stuck to the rules. All dangerous machinery had to be fenced.

Machines need power. This was usually transmitted by overhead spinning shafts which transmitted power from one pulley to another. These too needed guarding. I once went with a senior inspector to a factory where a young worker's clothes had got wrapped round the belt and spun him round the shaft to his death. It had stripped off all his clothes. One of the most gruesome tasks was the inspection of slaughter houses. A tough inspector who had been a paratrooper during the war told me it was the thing he most detested. They were supposed to be kept hygienic, but gore and guts were inevitably often too much in evidence.

Everyone has heard about the great Wedgwood pottery, but that had moved from its old quite elegant eighteenth century brick construction (it is now a museum in a park where once was a waste) to a modern factory at Barlaston south of the city. The city of Stoke is really a conglomeration of five towns, running from Burslem in the north down to Hanley, then Stoke itself and further still. The towns had been made famous in the novels of Arnold Bennett, the local boy destined to go to London as he put it in his early novel *The Man From The North*. He ended up living in Brighton and, having become a sophisticate, often staying in wicked Paris. His greatest novel is

Clayhanger, a family chronicle. It contains a memorable thought of the central character about growing old which, having grown old myself now, I can heartily endorse 'Something terrible has happened to the world since I was a boy.' The main industry of the town was pottery, and forty or so squat red brick bottle kilns giving off smoke from the so called 'pot banks' had replaced the tall slender mill chimneys of my East Lancashire youth. The workers lived in mean terraces, but here they were made of red brick rather than grey stone. I took lodgings in one. My landlady did my room and provided breakfast and dinner as the Oxford landladies had done. But what a totally different world I entered when I left the house. It might have been on a different planet rather than just in a different country. Arnold Bennett once said that when he passed the district by train in his later years he used to draw the curtains. My landlady had a son who went out to work. There was no man about the house. I think she may have been a widow. She was just at the transition stage from womanhood to middle age. She was a kindly soul and concerned for me having to be apart from my fiancée. I think the nature of my work puzzled her and also made her concerned for me because I was evidently not suited to it. It rather amused her son as well. People somehow have a sixth sense for these things.

I felt I must know more about factory work from the inside so to speak. I got talking to the nice owner of a small metal works I had gone to inspect, on this occasion unaccompanied, and asked him if I could come and help once a week. He kindly agreed and so I found myself learning to manage that fearful object a lathe, guard and all. I must have told the chief inspector about this for it was made clear to me in a gentle manner that it was improper for an inspector to enter into a relationship of this kind with a factory owner on the grounds of an inspector's need to be impartial. So my apprenticeship ended after a couple of weeks and the lathe remains a mystery.

I must now sketch some of my colleagues. The formidable but kindly chief inspector retired and was deservedly made a Dame of something or other in the Queen's honour list. Names are strange and for some reason I can't remember the name of her successor.

Like most inspectors he was not a local man. In fact he came from Kent where his father was, I think, the owner of a well-known paper mill. He was a tall dignified kindly man with a quiet but authoritative manner. I often accompanied him as his apprentice, so to speak. He could feel that I was unhappy in my work and always treated me with sympathy. Mr Fish was quite different. He was a short peppery man who had been a paratrooper in the war where he had entered combat from a crashed glider. Woe betide any German he met I thought. For some reason he always took his family holiday in Abersoch. I think he was married, but I never met his wife. It was he who detested inspecting abattoirs and, having been to one with him, I can see why. He made quite clear his contempt for me as a muff. I am not sure but I think he sometimes used to refer to me mockingly as 'the professor'. Such are the vagaries in minor cruelty of human nature!

The fourth inspector was completely different. His name was Victor Jordan. He was a small genial man always smiling. He too had been in the war. He had served in Fighter Command and flown Spitfires. I got to know him well because after my marriage I moved with Barbara to live in Madeley, a pretty village between Keele and Nantwich, the Cheshire town where my first son Matthew was born. Barbara and I were living by then in a caravan up the road from the mill. Across the village green was a lovely timbered Tudor mansion. Victor told me that Charles had hidden there for a spell when he was on the run from the parliamentarians after his defeat. So many places in England have civil war associations. There was even a battle of Nantwich. Victor and Barbara got on very well together and we sometimes invited him to the caravan for an evening meal. He was the only one of the inspectors who maintained contact after I left. He exchanged letters with Barbara. He had got married and had children. He once visited us at our home in Kent. Sadly, he died not long after that. He must have been about seventy.

At times I felt at such a dead end and so miserable that I would walk the dismal streets and wish I had the courage to make an end to it all by committing suicide. I think that this was the most miserable period of life that I had been through until the period following the suicide of my younger son Edward.

I must now backtrack. Sometime in 1957 or early 1958 when I had some leave and was staying in Slough I took Barbara to either Windsor or Henley and sealed our engagement with a diamond wedding ring. We were married, as I have said, at the parish church of Burnham near Slough close to the beautiful and famous Burnham Beeches. We went to Somerset for our honeymoon. We stayed at a beautiful farmhouse. The couple who ran the farm soon recognized that we were on honeymoon. We visited Alfoxden where Wordsworth and Coleridge had lived when they were writing the *Lyrical Ballads*. We visited the old cottage at Nether Stowey where Coleridge wrote 'This Lime Tree Bower.' We went to the beautiful old ruined castle of Kilve which was by the sea. The church clock there is mentioned in one of Wordsworth's poems. It was on our honeymoon that, after some initial shyness, a marriage, that was to last sixty-one years, was consummated.

15 MARRIED LIFE IN A CARAVAN. LIBRARY WORK IN THE UNIVERSITY OF KEELE.

At least in working as a factory inspector I was not 'sponging' on my mother. I was constantly looking round for a new job. I saw and advertisement for a post in the library of the University of Liverpool and applied. I was called to interview. The chief librarian was an old curmudgeon. In his case his name is well forgotten. He glared at me sarcastically across the table and said: 'You needn't think you are going to come here and read *Essays in Criticism* in the library instead of getting on with your work.'

Naturally I was not accepted. Later when I was working in the library at the University of Keele the genial chief librarian there, Stanley Stewart, told me the chief librarian in Liverpool University Library had a terrible reputation as a sour old soul. Apparently he used to go round the library scolding the girls who worked there till they burst into tears. Yet again I was struck as in the case of Mr Fish, with the petty malevolence which can inflict human beings.

I finally got a post as a cataloguer in the Library at the University of Keele. I think my salary as a factory inspector was about £600 a year. My library salary was about £400 a year, but it was salvation. I moved from

Hell to Paradise. For, as is said somewhere in *Piers Plowman* to be in a library is to be in paradise.

Where were we to live as a married couple? We could not afford to buy a house and renting was not so common then. The solution was a caravan but here again I had to turn to my mother for help with the deposit. I also had to pay a small rent to the farmer at Moor Hall Farm for a plot in the meadow where he grazed his cows. The meadow sloped upwards from the caravan to the farmhouse. On the other side was a hedge between us and the lane. It was about this hedge in the Spring thaw that I wrote one of my best poems. Even the fastidious poet and disciple of Ezra Pound the proud Northumbrian Basil Bunting was later to express his approval of it. It was about the quarrels which sometimes arise in early married life and had the title 'Quarrels'. I quote:

A gentler wind begins to strip
Slow melting snow
From darkening trees that drip
On leaf mould below.

Where branches cast a deeper shade
There is no thaw.
Though lips soothe wounds they made
The heart stays raw.

The caravan was twenty-two feet long. It had no running water and no electricity. As we had no water I had to get water from the wife of the farm labourer. The Machin family lived in an old cottage by the gate into the lane that led down to the village. The gate of course had always to be closed after one used it, as we did every morning when we both went to work. As we had no running water we had to use an Elsan lavatory in the back compartment. This was emptied each week by men who came round. Our heating was by oil lamps and a wooden stove vented though the roof. When it was freezing in the winter the caravan could get very cold, but when we got the stove going the opposite happened and by bedtime it was stiflingly hot. Our beds consisted of a bunk bed which we pulled down at night. It was very comfortable. There was no fence round the caravan and cows are full of curiosity. They loved to lick the caravan sides.

Eventually Mr Machin put a barbed wire fence round the caravan with a stile we could climb over. In time we had water and electricity laid on which greatly improved matters. We had a portable radio to listen to and we read aloud. It was at this time that I read the whole of *War and Peace* and *Anna Karenina* in Aylmer Maude's wonderful translation aloud to Barbara as we lay in the bunk.

As a qualified and experienced infant teacher Barbara had no difficulty in getting a job. One of the other teachers Norma Sherratt became a great friend and later on we often used to visit her and her husband Eric, who worked for the coal board, in their bungalow in the village of Endon. Later on they visited us when we had moved to Canterbury and were godparents to our son Matthew. Everyone in the school was amazed that someone had come of their own free will from the lovely south, as they saw it, to work in smoky Stoke.

Of course they understood why when they learned of our marriage. Every morning we would set off, carefully checking that we had left the gate to the grazing meadow closed, and catch the bus. I had a journey of about two miles to Keele, while Barbara had a journey about four times as long. I think she had to change at Newcastle Under Lyme. Then the bus went through Stoke up the hill past the old Wedgwood works to Hanley centre where the school was situated close to the theatre.

My period working as a cataloguer in the library at the University of Keele was a very happy one, particularly after what I had been through. I used to say goodbye to Barbara and get off the bus outside the Keele Arms and cross the road. Then I had about a quarter of an hour's walk along a pleasant lane flanked by houses in which some of the professors lived. The University of Keele was one of the first of the new universities and had opened around 1960. It had a four-year degree in which one could combine subjects, as the University of Kent was to do later.

Its most well-known teacher was probably Professor Flew who taught philosophy. He was an atheist and it was said upset some of his Christian students to such a degree that they became depressive. It was about this time that the Russians launched their sputnik with the astronaut Gagarin who encircled the globe. This was seen on television. Suddenly everyone seemed to be under the illusion that if one learned Russian one could be a space scientist or an astronaut. The Simon Langton Grammar school in Canterbury dropped Latin for Russian. I later got to know Nicholas Leader who taught my younger son Edward Russian there. When the University of Kent opened it was possible to have Russian language lessons. Not surprisingly, then, the University of Keele had appointed a Russian, a genial Scotsman called Jim Forsyth.

My interest in the Russian language had begun during the war, when, as a boy, I made my father proud by being able to pronounce the names of the Russian generals correctly. I had read many Russian classics by the time I was at Keele so I jumped at the chance when Jim Forsyth started an evening class in the Russian language. I wanted to be able to read Pushkin and Tolstoy in the original. The library at Keele was only just being built up towards to the 100,000 volumes it soon came to attain. It was located in the beautiful old manor house at that time. This had once been lived in by the exiled Russian Grand Duke Michael, a relative of the Tsar. The cataloguing room, which also contained the modern languages section which, of course, included Russian, was located at the rear of the house. It had a huge window which looked out on the lovely grounds sloping down towards a wood and lake at the bottom. There were reputed to be adders there. It was, in fact, curiously like a Russian country estate. This garden made a lovely walk for a summer lunch break. I made friends with the manager of the University bookshop and we used to take those walks together. When I left he thoughtfully made me a gift of a paperback copy of Pushkin's *Evgeny Onegin* in Russian. All four of us cataloguers sat by the huge bay windows opening out on to the garden.

I must say something about my colleagues. The chief cataloguer was a sprightly Jewish unmarried lady in her early forties or so. We always addressed her as Miss Friedman. She helped me with the rules of cataloguing. We used the classification system of the Library of Congress and had their complete catalogue in classifying a book. Classification has a philosophical aura about it for the world of books is the world in little, so to speak. Miss Friedman was fluent in German and had started to learn Russian. As she had a great gift for language learning she soon became more than adequate in it. She was naturally pleased when I started to learn Russian and let me catalogue the Russian books with her guidance.

There were two other cataloguers: Joan and Mary. They were both lovely in appearance and manner, but

Joan unfortunately had had some illness which left her face slightly disfigured. Perhaps partly because her name recalled my first love I was very attracted to Mary. On such things do affinities arise. I think they all four recognized my attraction to Mary and that Joan was slightly jealous as in Oxford Barbara's friend Sheila had been. But we all got on very well for the most part.

Barbara had the view very common at the time that the way to first getting to a man's heart and then keeping it was to be a good cook and, in particular, to bake excellent cakes and pastries. She was bold enough to agree to invite my cataloguing colleagues to dinner in the caravan. The dinner went very well. After it I walked them down to the bus stop. Women have very sensitive antennae in such matters and I think Barbara recognized my erotic attraction to Mary, but as nothing came of it marital piece was not disturbed. What the dispute was which led to my poem 'Quarrels' I cannot remember. Perhaps it was about my attraction to Mary/

Though I enjoyed my work in the library I still hankered for an academic job teaching English literature and kept a look out for posts in the *Times Literary Supplement* and the *Times Higher Educational Supplement*. Advertisements appeared for a post in Uganda and a post in New Zealand.

I applied for both. I had an interview for the post in Uganda and it was in fact offered to me. At the interview I met a very nice young man named Ron Tamplin who had earlier studied at Oxford where he developed a strong love for medieval literature. Perhaps he had been helped in this by the fact that he was an ardent Roman Catholic as was the Irish girl Anne whom he married. However I was informed that the posting had been cancelled. This was perhaps as well as Uganda was ruled at the time by the murderous dictator Idi Amin. With the aid of excellent references from my tutor Freddy Bateson and from J. A. W. Bennett the kind New Zealander who had written to me after I had failed the viva at Magdalen promising help, I was appointed as an Assistant Lecturer at the University of Canterbury in Christchurch on the south island of New Zealand. Its name was the reason the new university where I was later to teach had had to be called The University of Kent At Canterbury. There could not be two Universities Of Canterbury in the Commonwealth Universities Yearbook. So began a great three year adventure for Barbara and myself. It was in New Zealand that our first son Matthew was born. Our first-class fares for the outward journey were paid by the university. If we wanted to return we would have to pay our own fares. When we got on the boat there was Ron Tamplin with his wife Anne. Another of life's coincidences! He had been appointed to the University of Hamilton on the North Island. Another young man Ken Ruthven a Yorkshireman who had studied English Literature at Manchester University with the then prestigious Frank Kermode was also going to teach at Christ Church like me. At that time he had a deep interest in the American poet Wallace Stevens on whom he had done his doctorate. He had with him his beautiful young wife Rachel who came from County Durham. She had met Ken when she was reading history at the same university. She seemed to have been initiated into the subject as a young girl by reading the popular historical novels of Georgette. She had a slight and charming lilt in her voice.

I must explain why we had been paid for as first class passengers. At that time New Zealand was a great meat exporter to the United Kingdom. This was long before the changes brought about by the Common Market. The meat had to be carried in refrigerated holds. The Shaw Saville Line specialized in this. But this meant there was only space for forty passengers and to maximize returns these had all to pay first class fares. The other passengers were a party of doctors going to a medical conference in New Zealand. At dinner we could see them looking at us with a curiosity which betokened their wonder at how a party as young as ours could afford first class fares. I shall certainly never travel in such luxury again. We all had excellent and spacious cabins and a steward to lay out our best clothes before dinner each evening. The weather in the Bay of Biscay was horrendous and we rolled about in our cabins for days being seasick. Travelling first class did not save you from that, though we must have been a nuisance to the stewards. The distance to New Zealand is 14,000 miles. When we got into the Atlantic things calmed down. We had stops at Dutch Curacao and at Panama as we passed through the Panama canal. At one point in the Pacific we made a tour of the bridge and the captain told us that at that moment there was not a ship within a thousand miles. I did not know at the time that three years later Barbara and I would return to England on an Italian liner (formerly the British liner Kenya from the thirties) the Castel Felice. We soon named it the Castel Infelice because of its overcrowding. Still it enabled me to practice the Italian I had learned in New Zealand and it was delightful to glimpse something of Italy when we paused there to unload the many Italian immigrants who were either returning permanently or just visiting relatives. As we came back through the Suez canal, I can say that like Sir Francis Drake I have circumnavigated the globe.

16 TO NEW ZEALAND

My title is deliberately ambiguous as between the voyage to and a dedication to this wonderful country.

So in our long sea journey Barbara and I followed in the fictional footsteps of the young emigrants in Clough's poem *The Bothie of Tober-Na- Vuosich* and the real footsteps of the one hundred or so emigrants sponsored by the Anglican Church who went to found a settlement in Christchurch in the 1850's. Their names could be seen framed on the wall of Christchurch public library. One of the sponsors was Lord Lyttelton of Hagley Hall to the West of Birmingham. The beautiful park near the University in Christchurch was named Hagley Park after him. In my work on Matthew Arnold I had come across the unhappy story of his brother Tom. He went out to New Zealand hoping to work as a school inspector in the 1860's. Unhappy in his work he then tried farming from a position of total inexperience and naturally failed at that. Unhappily, considering he was the son of a militant Church of England man, he eventually converted to Roman Catholicism under the influence of the Newmanism still present in Oxford. I would never consider converting to an institution I believe one of the most malign to have dominated human life, along with the Ayatollahs and the Russian Communist party. Still let us turn away our eyes from such matters, as Dante says,

We arrived in Auckland, which seemed largely to consist of bungalows and then travelled by train to Wellington. We took the ferry across the straits to the South Island. From Wellington we took another ferry to

Lyttelton Harbour near Christchurch and then on to the small township of Governors Bay. It was early February and in the middle of summer. We were taken to the home of one of the professors, Winston Rhodes and his delightful wife Sophie. They were giving a party to the English department. To recur to Dante, we and thought we had reached the earthly paradise. The garden with its orange trees and other exotica sloped in terraces down towards the bay.

As the ocean had filled the crater of a volcano the water was deep enough to take a modern cruise ship, not then in vogue, or even an ocean liner, though, of course there were no docks. The bay is separated from Christchurch by the Cashmere Hills. I think the tunnel under them was built later so we were taken over the pass by car. Christchurch was a bit of a shock after that. The exotica and the almost Mediterranean ambience had completely disappeared.

We had lodgings in Amherst street in a small wooden bungalow with a large garden with apple and pear trees in it. Our landlady was a kind and charming widow whose son would regularly visit her. The bungalow was arranged so we had a self-contained section. It was about a mile to the city centre using a road which ran beside the grassy banks of the river Avon. Then from the centre it was a further mile or so to the English department. This was situated quite close to a private school (I think our landlady's son may have taught there) and to the entrance to Hagley Park a spacious park not unlike the one in North Oxford.

I must now say something about my colleagues. The head of department was a Canadian, called John Garrett. He, like all the staff, was most welcoming. He invited us to a party at his house so we could get to know the other staff. I remember he made what I thought at the time as an ingenuous young lecturer was a very cynical remark. We were by some well filled bookshelves and he pointed to them and said: ' Do you know what all these people are saying?' Innocently I answered 'No.' Then adopting a plaintive tone he repeated: 'Listen to me. Listen to me.' Now I see he perhaps had a point. Does not Nietzsche ask plaintively: *'Hoert niemand mir zu?'* 'Is anybody listening?'

Professor Rhodes had, I think, been head of department for a spell, but was now one among the other professors. As I have said he was a most kind man. There was a rumour that he had once had a certain notoriety as a communist and republican. I think that, like many duped innocents such as the Webbs, he had visited the Soviet Union in the dreadful thirties. If so, it is quite likely that he opposed New Zealand's entry into the war while the Hitler Stalin pact was in effect, changing his mind, of course, after Hitler invaded Russia in 1941.

Perhaps the most friendly member of staff of all was a tall handsome man named Ray Copeland, by then a professor too I think, or perhaps that came later. He and his charming wife invited us to a delightful summer afternoon garden party.

I was particularly attracted to him, because, like my brother Bobby, he had been in Bomber Command during the war. I was struck by his saying that his biggest fear still gave him nightmares. It was surviving a crash, but then being unable to get clear of the wreckage and so burned alive.

George Turner taught Old English and even Old Norse to those who wished to specialize in the language. He was also very interested in the discipline of Linguistics which we sometimes discussed. This gave his discourse something of a philosophical tinge. I did not know any of the philosophy department which had a certain degree of prestige because Professor Karl Popper had taught there during the war when he was writing *The Open Society*. However as my philosophical interests somewhat overlapped with metaphysics and the philosophy of religion I was pleased to have discussions with one of the theologians there. It was about this time the the paradoxical death Of God theology was popular. The University of Christchurch organized every summer a summer school at Curious Cove a bay in the north of the South Island It was only accessible from the sea. My wife and I took our baby Matthew there in his second year. As he was just by then at the age when he had begun to crawl, he evinced the limitless exploratory curiosity of babies and we had the greatest difficulty in keeping away from the unsavoury areas where trash was dumped. It was at this summer School that I had many conversations about linguistics with George Turner and attended lectures on the new theology with members of the theology department with whom I discussed it.

There was some sort of competition among the students in public speaking and one of the students contributed by reading aloud the whole of Edward Fitzgerald's *The Rubaiyat Of Omar Khayya*m' humour of the students came out when they awarded him 'The Travelling Fellowship In Poetry Reading'.

The University of Christchurch had a Russian department of two. The Professor was a benign old man whose name was De Laberbis. As he had fought for Kolchak's White army in the Civil War, he had had to flee to Harbin with his wife after their defeat. When Mao came to power ther had had to flee a second time this time landing in safe New Zealand. Their assistant was a remarkable man called Alex Lozhkin. He spoke fluently French, German, Russian and Italian. This meant I could continue Russian lessons with him. I also sat in on his lectures on Russian literature, but these largely consisted of a dry recitation of the names and dates of the lives and works of Russian poets and prose writers from Derzhavin in the eighteenth century to the twentieth century. He did not give us an appreciative criticism whatsoever. He rather scorned my admiration for Tolstoy. He was a Dostoevskyan rather than a Tolstoyan, to use the time old division.

Barbara and I used to speculate about his origins. The name Lozhkin certainly sounded Russian. We thought he had perhaps fled Communist Russia and got to France perhaps, and then was put to forced labour by the Germans. He once made the cryptic remark that the war had looked very different from the other side of the channel. I wondered whether he had been a forced labourer on the V1 flying bomb sites in Normandy and had been bombed by us. But he gave no details and his reticence made curiosity seem impertinent. He seemed a dyed in the wool bachelor, but started courting the best of his students of Russian and married her after we had left New Zealand. I think they had children. He and De Laberbis were rather wary in their behaviour to each other. I was once invited to Professor De Laberbis's home and met Madame De Laberbis. She paid a compliment to my attempts at spoken Russian and had the rather languid air of a pre-revolutionary lady from St.Petersburg who might burst into hysterics at any moment. Perhaps listening to them both had some effect on my pronunciation of Russian, for, many years later I got into conversation with some Russians I met by chance on a train to London, and they told me that I spoke with an old fashioned St. Petersburg accent.

Ken Ruthven and I got on very well with the students. In my first year I taught an introductory course on the metaphysical poets which I very much enjoyed. The only example of nationalism I came across was when a student asked why we weren't rather studying New Zealand poets. But she asked very politely. I also earned a little extra money by the tedious tasks of marking university entrance papers. The occasional 'howler' amused, as when a student wrote of Jane Austen's novel *Emma:* 'After her nine climaxes Emma is a changed woman.'

The salary of an assistant lecturer was, if I remember rightly, £800 a year going up after three years, if you were promoted to lecturer, to £1000. We always tried to put enough money aside for the trip home if I could get a post in England. My mother sent me the TLS every week and I scoured it for posts.

We liked New Zealand very much. All four of us decided to go up to the North Island to see Ron and Ann Tamplin who were at the University of Hamilton.

Ken Ruthven was an excellent cyclist and we both used to cycle to work. I was very grateful Barbara had taught me in Oxford. I had a sleek modern bike but, to my surprise he brought an old iron 'Boanerges' as we named it. It had no brakes on the handlebars. I think you braked by back-pedalling furiously. At weekends we used to ride out to the Cashmere Hills for exercise. When it came to going downhill, I rode very cautiously while Ken disappeared in the distance at breakneck speed. Barbara also had a cycle to get to school. In winter it might be freezing in the bungalow, so she piled on the clothes, but when it warmed up and she returned in the afternoon she got into a terrible sweat. When her pregnancy with our elder son Matthew became more and more evident, I used to worry about her cycling.

I could drive so we hired a mini I to go up the North Island. We had a puncture driving past one of the three spectacular volcanoes on the way. Curiously instead of deflating the tire inflated. There were the most wonderful fern forests on the which we walked through. There was no fear of snakes for there were none in New Zealand unlike in Australia. The legend was that a sharp eye was kept on the hawsers of any boat in dock that had come from Australia in case any snakes crawled down from them on to the land. In the North Island we, of course, visited the spectacular steaming mud pools and saw a geyser spout. While still on the South Island we had already watched a party of Maoris do their fearsome haka. New Zealand was fortunate in being able to generate electricity from naturally produced steam. I very much wanted to visit the spectacularly beautiful Bay of Plenty, but we did not manage that. We did go to a university camping hut in the southern alps which was near the 3,000-foot-high Arthur' pass over to Hokitika with its fern forests and coal mines on the West coast. When we got to the hut it was bitter cold, but we managed to get the log stove going. We were on our own and just about getting to sleep when eight burly New Zealanders piled into the hut. New Zealand has a great variety of birds, some of which are unique to the islands. There were rather famous flightless black ones called kiers which squawked very loudly and haunted the rubbish tips. One day Barbara and I climbed to the top of the pass and walked down to Hokitika which was a very strange place reputed to have 400 inches of rain in a year. Luckily it did not rain while we were there.

What one misses in New Zealand is the wonderful architecture of old Europe, as the islands were settled by Europeans so recently. We used to walk in Hagley park pushing Matthew in his pram and look west at the Cashmere Hills. It was all very beautiful and peaceful (this was the time of the Cuban missile crisis) but we longed to be back home. Barbara was so nostalgic that she listened to the Archers which was obtainable on New Zealand radio. We had moved from our first lodgings to lodgings in a beautiful wooden two storey house with a vine growing over the verandah. It was situated just off the Papanui road. The hospital just down the road was where Matthew was born. I fear our house cannot have survived the devastating earthquake on Tuesday February 22 2011which destroyed so much of the city. Our dear landlady miss Field was seventy years old and had never been outside New Zealand, yet, to our astonishment, she still referred to England as 'home'. We felt having a baby playing round the house was getting on her nerves so we moved to a rented wooden bungalow which was much less pleasant. native New Zealanders of English origin wanted to remain there, but still felt a strong impulse to see the cultural treasure house which was Europe. In particular Italy with its wonderful legacy of art and architecture had a great attraction. If they made the long journey to Europe they certainly wanted to see the great cities of Tuscany, Florence, Siena and Pisa. This brings me back to Alex Lozhkin. He offered Italian lessons. He was a very skilled language teacher and used hand outs which, after basic grammar, contained passages from Italian literature. So we all read some Dante Petrarch Leopardi and the most famous

Italian novelist Manzoni the author of *I Promessi Sposi The Betrothed*. On the return journey home on the insalubrious Italian boat I was to read the whole book with the aid of a dictionary. Strangely my Italian connected with my

Russian, because Alex gave me a typed copy of an essay on symbolism by the scholarly Russian poet and critic Vyacheslav Ivanov from the *Enciclopedia Italiana*. It was particularly interesting because Ivanov made a distinction between what one might call the upward transcendental symbolism of Dante and the downward immanent symbolism of a decadent and Satanist such as the Baudelaire familiar from my school. Furthermore Alex was particularly impressed by the Italian scholar and critic of Russian literature Ettore Lo Gatto. When I visited Italy later on I bought Lo Gatto's book on Russian literature and his book on Soviet literature as well.

At last I saw an advertisement for a post in English literature at the University of Glasgow. I applied and the answer was favourable. The longsuffering Freddy Bateson was called upon for yet another reference and this was not to be the last, for Kent was to come. Of course an interview was out of the question and there was no zooming then. By an extraordinary piece of luck the young Shakespeare scholar at Glasgow David Bank was a New Zealander and was visiting Christ Church. He was asked to size me up and sent back a dispatch even shorter than Julius Caesar's. It simply said: 'Greenwood all right'. I was later to lodge with David in his palatial rented mansion off the Great West Road where we consumed copious draughts of whisky. When Barbara and Matthew joined me from her parents' house in Slough we moved to lodgings in the city.

17 TWO YEARS IN GLASGOW

So after a spell in Slough with Barbara's parents and visiting my mother and sister I settled in digs near Partick Thistle. Our landlady was a Mrs McConochie a dear old soul who adored Matthew who was still at the crawling stage, but would soon begin to toddle. His favourite pastime was to crawl into her kitchen cupboard where he would play with the pots and pans. Barbara had found a job at a primary school in the city and was finding it difficult to cope with the strong local dialect spoken by the children.

Glasgow was, of course notorious for its slums, the high ancient tenement blocks of the Gorbals, and for the drunkenness in Sauchie Hall street after dark. It is of course a splendid city with fine town hall and the world famous Rennie art gallery which was later to be devastated by a severe fire. There was also the Kelvingrove art gallery on the northern outskirts of the city. The university itself was located in a splendid neo-Gothic building from which a lofty tower arose. It possessed a large chapel. It also had a large and excellent library with open access and borrowing allowed.

Unlike in England, some study of English literature went back there to the eighteenth century. One of its most famous professors was Adam Smith the founder of economics and the author of the splendid, but rather neglected, *The Nature of Sympathy*. He also gave lectures on rhetoric. His papers were being edited by a member of staff, Hannah Buchan. Most of the members of the English staff were at this time from

England. Scottish nationalism. This was despite the efforts of the poet Hugh McDiarmid who combined the incompatibles of Soviet Marxism and nationalism. The English included Professor Butter a specialist on the work of Edwin Muir who had previously been a professor at Edinburgh. Every year in the summer vacation the two English departments would meet for lunch half way between the towns. Both Mark Kinkead-Weekes, originally from South Africa, whom I have mentioned before, and Ian Gregor were teaching at Edinburgh at that time. Both later became heads of department at the University of Kent and so colleagues of mine.

The most widely known figure at the University of Glasgow was the poet Edwin Morgan. He sometimes wrote so called concrete poetry in the form of shaped figures such as eggs or vases popular in Tudor times. To me it was an utterly trivial pursuit. However, he amassed a large body of serious work and his *Collected Poems* was received with great acclaim. Homosexuality was illegal at the time and could be punished by imprisonment, so Edwin was what was then known as a 'closet homosexual'. So well did he keep his secret hat not even his best friend Jack Rillie knew of it till after his death. Barbara was very moved by a poem by him which describes a clandestine rapid encounter with a fellow homosexual in a Glasgow urinal.

Jack Rillie was the member of staff with whom I formed the closest friendship. He had organized an evening discussion group on matters philosophical and theological. It was to this group that I gave the paper 'Poetry and Paradise' which among other mystic poets discussed Ibn Arabi and the Persian Jelalludin Rumi. It was later published in the January 1967 issue of *Essays In Criticism*.

As in Oxford, teaching was done in lectures, seminars and single supervisions and I was involved in all these forms. I was assigned to give a set of lectures introductory to English literature to the first year students in a large steeply raked lecture hall. There must have been over 200 students looking down on me. The first year students had the reputation of noisily rolling pennies down the aisles if the lecture bored or in any way offended them, so I approached my task with great trepidation. No pennies were rolled, but it may be that the custom had died out. In one seminar I had a very pretty girl student who was always smiling and cheerful called Kate McCluskie. She was a brilliant student who got first class honours. She had been to my friend David Banks's Shakespeare class. Later she became head of the English department at Kent, a position I was rather glad never to have attained because it involved so much administration and I hated administration. So I was in the piquant position of being an underling to a one time pupil. I was to find the Shakespeare specialists at Kent a strange bunch. Initially the Shakespeare course had been compulsory for all part two English students, much to my approval. The specialists abolished this. It may have been because they only wanted students who were motivated to study Shakespeare rather than compelled to do so.

I now come to a striking example of what Wittgenstein has taught us to call aspect change as when, to use his example, we discover that what we have previously seen as the drawing a duck can flip over into being the drawing of a rabbit. I was teaching an evening class in town about modern poetry, using an anthology. Ted Hughes's poem 'The Thought Fox' about a poem appearing on the page, was then in vogue. It was widely admired and I too was one of its admirers. I drew attention to what I thought were its felicities when suddenly one of the students tore it to pieces saying it was a fake. Suddenly I saw what he was getting at. Ever since I have regarded Ted Hughes as one of the most overrated poets of the twentieth century, trading on a false Laurentian primitivism which is far from the real article.

Now comes the meta critical problem. Was this nothing more than an exchange of persuasive rhetoric in which his rhetoric happened to be the more persuasive? Was there any objective warrant completely standing outside our respective sensibilities which guaranteed that one of us was right and the other wrong. But critical judgements, unlike those in physics are and must be rooted in the sensibility if they are to be sincere. Thus the problem stands and always will. We are convinced that some judgements are better than others but, as Kant showed in the first part of his *Critique Of Judgement*, we can only appeal for consensus. Kant of course believed that such judgements would involve universal agreement, just like ethical judgements. Nietzsche was perhaps disconcertingly nearer the mark when he confidently asserted his judgements were superior to those of others because his taste was superior which philosophers would regard as a non-sequitur. This does not mean that it might not be true.

I have mentioned that Scottish Nationalism was not nearly so widespread then as it is now. The one student I had who evinced it used to come to the tutorial with me ostentatiously wearing the kilt. I don't remember any other students doing so at that time. He was somewhat reticent and always polite. I think we read Burns together which was probably good for my understanding of Burns's demotic. His nationalism was confined to an observation similar to that of my New Zealand student, though made much less aggressively.

Why did we not read more Scottish literature he mildly expostulated on one occasion.

By a strange coincidence, if I remember rightly, Jim Forsyth my Russian teacher at Keele, had come to Glasgow, so I was able to continue Russian lessons with him.

One of the drawbacks to Glasgow was what seemed to me, after New Zealand's sunshine, its appalling constant dark cloud and rainfall. This meant that one made the most of the few fine sunny days we got. I remember one when there wasn't a cloud in the sky we decided to motor to the beautiful Loch Lomond. On the way we stopped at an isolated house serving tea. There was a kind of allegory of the dominance of the motor car in the twentieth century in that, when we asked about the significance of the horseshoe over the door, we were told that, in addition to being a traditional good luck sign, a story about the house lay behind it. In the past it had been a smithy and one day the blacksmith had happened to walk out into the road and been killed by a passing car. *'Sic transit.'*

Mrs McConochie was as loving as a grandma to Matthew and he must have started to speak early for I seem to remember hearing him call her granny. However we thought her having to look after him all day while we were at work was getting too much for her and that we must try to buy a house. We found one out beyond the posh stone houses of Milngavie. It was part of a new estate and at the top of Cruachan Road. A co-op store was conveniently located at the foot of the road. To the north over the fields was Hadrian's wall. We travelled to work by bus and Barbara had to manage the pram on the bus and take Matthew with her to work. The bus to the city passed along the Great West road with splendid houses in one of which I had lodged with David Banks on arrival. If one took the other direction towards Loch Lomond we passed a little way out depressingly tall tower blocks. There was not a single shop or pub or cinema or cafe. We could not imagine how a City Council could create such an abomination of desolation. Barbara's parents now had a car and came up to visit us. One day we went to the seaside at Helensborough. It bucketed rain all the time we were there. As I had found when I had a day out from school with my mother there is nothing more dismal and depressing than a seaside resort on a dark rainy day.

By this time the financial situation of my mother and sister had greatly improved. I think they had got some capital together by selling their large house in Nelson. They moved first to a semi in Newcastle Under Lyme and then to a bungalow in the pleasant village of Shavington between Newcastle Under Lyme and Keele. This was to be nearer to us, for we were still living in the caravan in Madeley at the time. It also had the tremendous advantage for my sister Edith in that it brought her near to Keele and she managed to enrol for a degree there so allowing her the university education she had missed in her girlhood. She thoroughly enjoyed university life and, if I remember rightly, eventually became President of the Student Union in time to meet Princess Margaret who was visiting as the Chancellor of the university. I may be confusing this with a degree day visit.

As I recounted earlier, Mark Kinkead-Weekes came to Glasgow to give a lecture on Kipling and invited me to apply for a post at the newly opened University of Kent at Canterbury. Both he and Ian Gregor were part of a move of Englishmen from the so-called 'Celtic Fringe' back south to the new universities just opening. I must mention two others, I think Maurice Larkin had been in Glasgow and made the move to Kent where he became a distinguished professor of modern history. Kent was to have an excellent history department.

As the university had a four-year degree at the start it encouraged cross disciplinary study and Maurice was very interested in French nineteenth century literature and the way French authors struggled with the problem of determinism raised by the scientific world view. The problem also affected Mrs Gaskell and George Eliot and the great Russian nineteenth century authors.

Out of his admirable lectures he published a fine book *Man And Society In Nineteenth-Century Realism: Determinism And Literature.*

Another lecturer who moved to Kent was Guido Almansi. Barbara and I had dinner with him and his wife Maria in his flat in the city which had a wonderful view over the city. He kindly helped me to keep up with my conversational Italian. Like many Italian men he was something of a philanderer and a witty colleague once gave him the sobriquet 'Phallus In Wonderland.'

I was interviewed in Canterbury and appointed to the post of Senior Lecturer In English And American Literature as the department was then called. It is now called The School Of English. The university had rented from the council some pleasing semis in a quiet area called Somner Close near to the city cemetery of all places where the hundred or so killed in one of the notorious so-called Baedeker raids were buried. Before starting I had during the summer break my first jaunt to America. I had got a post in the summer school at the University of Buffalo. My second visit to America was to be for much longer, a year with my family at the delightful University of Santa Barbara in California.

18 FIRST VISIT TO THE UNITED STATES: BUFFALO

Barbara was now pregnant with a second child whom we were to christen Edward Eliot, the Edward after me and the Eliot after George Eliot and, of course, T.S.Eliot, so, while I went off to America, she stayed with my mother and sister in Shavington and her baby was born in Nantwich hospital. I detested flying and managed to book a return passage on the Queen Elizabeth which was still plying the Atlantic. When we docked after seeing the world-famous Statue Of Liberty, I shared a taxi into New York City. I remember seeing the well-known skyscrapers towering in the distance and my companion muttered something like 'They never cease to be a wonder!' I saw some of the sights in my brief stay and, of course, like most visitors, ascended the Empire State Building. I remember wandering down some residential streets with the El railway above and wondering if I might meet my first love Mary, now married to an American. But I had no address and I even wondered if she might be dead.

Americans are fond of short-haul flights and Buffalo was four hundred miles to the north near the Canadian border but my fear of flying led me to take a Greyhound bus which for some reason seemed to be a form of transport despised by the American middle class. We had a couple of rest stops on the way. I was enchanted by the beauty of the countryside. Buffalo itself is an industrial city, but the university campus was well to the north of the city and had in front of it a pleasant expanse of green at the opposite side of which were some nice shops and cafes. There were several of us teachers over from England and they included Basil Bunting the Northumbrian poet who was undergoing something of fame at the time because he had just published his autobiographical poem *Briggflatts*. He had spent many years in Persia and fallen in love with the country and naturally, with its leading poet Firdousi the author of the *Shahnameh*. He expatiated eloquently on the beauty and freedom of Persian girls. The ayatollahs were not then in sight.

When we arrived we were all surprised and delighted that each of us had been given a graduate assistant to help with preparing photocopies we might want to use and also with the tedious task of grading. But, as far as I recall, not one of these assistants was male. The inevitable followed in those heady days of the 60s an 'inevitable' which would no longer be so in these politically correct days. Summer affairs began to blossom and develop in the knowledge that they would all be temporary. I had a charming assistant and she invited me out to her flat which was located in a nice house a little to the north in the countryside. Almost at once she started to undress as if this was expected of her as part of her duties as a graduate assistant and we made violent love.

The leading light at Buffalo was professor Leslie Fiedler who wrote for *Hudson Review* which, along with *Partisan Review* was one of the better critical journals of the time combining literary reviews with political commentary. This was a decade after the Hiss and Rosenberg scandals with the exposure of the naivety of many American liberals about Stalinism. It was also a decade after McCarthy's populist anti-communism with its proneness to identify all intellectuals as reds. Fiedler had collected some of his excellent essays on these matters in *An End to Innocence* published in 1952. I remember his remarking at a staff meeting how young we all seemed to him.

A lively young member of the staff was Arthur Efron who produced a periodical taking its cue from Cervantes's Sancho Panza. I contributed an article to it. I was briefly to talk with him on my way home from my second visit to America in 1968.

We visitors all got on well. One was the poet Tony Connor who was being published at the time. We used to meet for coffee and for evening meals in the café across the way which I mentioned. One of the highlights of our visit was a coach trip to Niagara Falls which quite lived up to its reputation as a sight well worth seeing. I was to visit again along with Barbara in 1968 on our way back home. I think there was a lot of licensed drug taking on the campus. I have never been able to understand why people can willingly damage our greatest gift, the reason which distinguishes us from the animals, by putting dangerous substances into themselves.

One of the visitors who was somewhat aloof was the Northumbrian poet Basil Bunting. I was later to get to know him much better when Barbara and I were in California for a year at the same time as he was, namely in 1968, another of the coincidences of my life. As a good Poundian I think he rather despised academe. Like Eliot he regarded Pound as '*il miglior fabbro*' 'the better craftsman,' Dante's compliment to Cavalcanti. However he had no time for Eliot's Anglicanism, rightly to my mind. His 'teaching' as far as |I could discover, consisted in reading aloud portions of Pound's *Cantos*. He admired the poetry while finding its Fascist ideology repellent. As we know from

Briggflatts Bunting was brought up as a Quaker and so was a conscientious objector in the Second World War. I got the impression that he may have done intelligence work for our secret service when he was in Persia however. He expatiated eloquently on the beauty and freedom of Persian girls. The abominable ayatollahs were not yet in sight.

It was during the sixties that the Beat poets were in vogue. There was a cult of Allen Ginsberg's 'Howl' which affected to lament the victims of the drug cult while at the same time exalting its glamour and seeing them all as *poetes maudits* accursed geniuses. It was hysterical rhetoric rather than poetry. This was a time in which it seemed everyone could be a genius, particularly in San Francisco, even if only for five minutes. The disaster of the Vietnam War from which many students claimed deferment played a role In the background to all this. Then there was the awful massacre of student protesters at Kent State University which occurred after my return to England. All this helped boost the Beats. Donald M Allen had produced a widely read anthology of their poetry *The New American Poetry* which was published by Grove Press in 1960. As well as 'Howl' selections from Charles Olson, Gary Snyder and Robert Creeley were also included in the anthology. The latter refers in one of his poems to 'The unsure egoist' as 'not good for himself'. All these poets were egoists far too pleased with themselves.

At the end of the book various statements on poetics were printed. The most famous and influential one was Charles Olson's account of the open field composition of what he called 'projective verse'. He partly looked back to Pound and characterized Milton's blank verse as a 'falling off' after the Elizabethans. It was clear that he looked to be the Ezra of the new poetry, as if the manifestos of the old one had not been preposterous enough. The syllable we were told connected to the head while the line connected to the heart. Much was mysteriously and mystically made of the breath. It was breath, not *logos* or reason (this came second) which was 'man's special qualification as animal.' Do we then breathe differently from the animals? We were in the world of a wizard of Oz. Olson an egoist of the first water like all the rest proclaimed the end of 'the individual as ego' in favour of something called 'Objectivism'. Eliot was repudiated at the close in the act of a good pseudo-Poundian. When I got to Kent I became friends with a young poet, Michael Grant, who was very intelligent, but who paid weird homage to this now mercifully forgotten nonsense.

I cannot remember what I taught, but I think I tried to introduce the students to some modern English poets, in particular Philip Larkin. I think my graduate assistant did a roneo copy of his wonderful 'Church Going' and that the students responded to this wise poem with appreciation.

My graduate assistant knew I was married and a father. She herself was engaged to a Lebanese whom I met on one occasion. I think she felt uneasy about my intentions and the relationship, and we only made love twice in the six weeks I was there, and she did not invite me to her flat as she had done before. We met for a meal occasionally. I much enjoyed my visit to her parents' farm. They were very charming, but I sensed a certain distrust on their part. Her father was a typical American in his love for guns and I enjoyed engaging in shooting too. But again, like the members of the gun lobby, he demurred when I said that guns were too easily available in America. His daughter also enjoyed shooting. I must mention that she made me much more knowledgeable about and appreciative of the poetry of Robert Frost. Frost was her favourite poet.

After I returned to England we corresponded for a while, but then the correspondence ceased. I did see her again when she visited England with her fiancé or husband, I can't remember which. He was not the Lebanese I had met, but a rather older man. When he greeted me he said to both of us: 'I can see there is a past here' intimating that he felt we had much to talk about, so he left us for a while. We had a meal and some conversation and then she went off to meet him again and go to the theatre together.

I think we have to acknowledge that a husband often has an affair when he is away from home or even when his wife is pregnant. This can sometimes wreck a marriage, for wives have antennae which immediately detect such things. Barbara and I went through a difficult patch, but, once the wounds healed, fortunately came out stronger. After all, if a husband is in the need of an affair, it shows he is not sufficient to himself, but needs support. A marriage and children give that support.

19 MY FIRST YEAR AT THE UNIVERSITY OF KENT AND A SURVEY OF THE STUDY OF ENGLISH AT KENT

I arrived at the University of Kent for Michaelmas Term 1966 and entered Rutherford College. The University had opened in 1965, the same year as The University of Sussex, with one college Eliot College named after the poet. In the second year when I arrived Rutherford College, named after the famous physicist from New Zealand was opened. In design it was a mirror image of the octagonal layout of Eliot College. Both were designed by the distinguished architect Sir Basil Spence who had designed the new Coventry cathedral. In the following two years we had Darwin College and Keynes College. Much later when the college system had fallen into disuse Woolf College was founded. The post of master no longer exists.

I must first say something about the college structure and then about the academic programme. The college structure was an imitation of the one at Oxford. In each octagon there were lecture rooms and seminar rooms and a teacher's room to give tutorials in, adjacent to which there were seven student bedrooms. I was assigned to NW4 (North West 4) a room I retained all my time at Kent. The colleges were co-educational, but female and male students were assigned different corridors. There were female cleaners and bedmakers for the students. Each member of staff was called on to be the moral tutor of a half dozen or so students as in Oxford. He was supposed to monitor the student's academic record and advise the student about any moral problems.

It was characteristic of the new universities to have a programme of interdisciplinary studies which included combining subject areas. In order to facilitate this, the degree course was for four years of three terms each. Every humanities student had to spend the first four terms on an area of study known as 'Britain and the Contemporary World' in which European literature, history and philosophy were combined. The course was taught through lectures, seminars and individual tutorials just as in the Oxford system. When students had passed the examinations at the end they were admitted to part two. Here it was still possible to combine two subjects if the student wished. A student could do English and Philosophy, say, or English and History or English and French, or alternatively elect to do a single subject degree. In the first two terms a seminar group of students might have three teachers in the seminar, in the case of English two English teachers and one Philosophy teacher or the reverse, one English teacher and two Philosophy teachers. This often happened in my case for I might be teaching the nature of literary criticism with Colin Radford, who alas died young, or the brilliant Frank Cioffi about whom I shall have more to say later. One of the first year humanities courses was a course on the English and European nineteenth century novel in which Flaubert's *Madame Bovary* and my favourite novel Tolstoy's *Anna Karenina* figured as well as Mrs Gaskell's *North and South* and George Eliot's *Middlemarch*. This laid the groundwork for my book *Tolstoy: The Comprehensive Vision* which appeared in

1975. I dedicated the book to Frank Cioffi because I had profited so much from discussions with him.

We of course attended each other's lectures. Frank Cioffi's introductory lectures to philosophy were particularly stimulating and recruited a lot of students for part two, some of whom might have been disillusioned as no teachers had his brilliance. Later the philosophy department recruited two excellent teachers Sean Sayers, who had studied at Cambridge University, having moved from physics to philosophy, and Richard Norman. Both played a considerable part in my later development. Richard with his lecture on Nietzsche's *Genealogy of Morals* and Sean in his working through all three of Kant's critiques with a group of enthusiasts.

The professor of French, Bob Gibson, was a genial character and a most amusing lecturer. I remember his beginning his lecture on Proust with the words 'I am going to try to show you that Proust isn't all balls'. Bill and Sheila Bell had come from the Celtic Fringe, in their case Edinburgh, to teach French at Kent and became great friends. There were also Maurice Larkin whom I have already mentioned for his first year lectures on the nineteenth century novel, Dick Crampton who was particularly interested in Russian history and from whom I learned a lot about it and the ebullient yet refined Richard Langhorne who gave excellent lectures on the causes leading to the outbreak of the First World War were leading lights in the History Department. Richard succeeded Professor Cameron as master of Rutherford college. His wife taught in the English Department.

When the university opened, its now capacious library building had not even been started and the faculty and I think the senate meetings were held in a fine old eighteenth century house in the town just to the north of the fourteenth century West Gate Tower. The library, which was being built up, was situated in a house on campus which later became the Registry. The University had three faculties the Humanities, the Natural Sciences and the Social Sciences. The Social sciences had some distinguished staff including Dick Scase, David Frisby, the expert on the German philosopher Georg Simmel whose formidable work on money he translated and David Crabtree. The natural scientists I did not know except for Professor Jack Powles who ran the Physics department. We later lived next door to the one time old Beverley farmhouse where he and his wife Jill lived, the proverbial Jack and Jill. She was later to give French lessons to our younger son Edward who went on to study the subject at Wadham College Oxford. They never seemed to do have any repairs done to either the interior or exterior of the old house, so later tenants had to do a complete renovation.

The head of the English Department was Professor R.A.Foakes a lively dapper man who had served in the R.A.F. during the war. This later led to a piquant situation during the student troubles of 1968 when he was barred from getting to his study by students who called him a Fascist. Anyone less Fascistic than this benevolent man could hardly be imagined. He took an interest in the work of all his staff and encouraged them all. He was particularly helpful to me in that he got me the contract to write the British Council pamphlet on the criticism of F.R. Leavis which was published by Longmans in their Writers and their Work series in 1978. Dennis Enright the poet, who was a friend of Frank Cioffi's, and who had connections with the British Council, forwarded to me a letter of protest Leavis's wife the waspish Queenie Leavis had written to the Council. In it she wrote: 'Who is this evident nonentity Edward Greenwood who dares to pronounce on my husband's life and work. She did not recognize that the phrase evident nonentity is an oxymoron. She probably had not read the pamphlet as it was, in fact full of admiration for her late husband's work Both the Leavis's hated the British Council and it was perhaps its imprimatur which had provoked her rage.

Other early members of the department were the wife of Richard Langhorne, a New Zealander called Roger Hardy who was our Chaucer specialist a voluble Americanist called Robert Lee who had married a southern Belle. Someone unkindly remarked that they had forgotten to put the clapper in. They soon divorced however and he married a Spanish girl, later going to teach English literature in Spain. He had a good knowledge of Spanish. He also had a sense of humour which he exercised on the topic of the sometimes slightly pompous Roger Hardy. One of his comic anecdotes concerned his having his suitcase opened by a customs officer when he was entering America. A pile of contraceptives ('rubbers' in American English) poured out and the custom's officer exclaimed: 'What are you, some kind of pervert?'. I have already mentioned Michael Grant, an extraordinarily handsome young man, the son of a Hull fisherman who I think may have died by drowning. He had had a book of poetry published and we often discussed poetry. He admired some of the American poets I earlier dismissed as frauds. We also discussed the philosophy of Wittgenstein in which both of us had developed a puzzled interest.

She was quite attractive, extremely slim and petite. She was also an ardent Roman catholic, so her name was very appropriate. Professor Cameron, the master of Rutherford was also a Roman Catholic and encouraged their courtship. Michael, for some obscure reason, had developed an interest in the Russian Orthodox Church. He even went up to London each weekend to attend Orthodox services in Kensington. Along with this developed an interest in Russian poetry in translation, particularly that of Osip Mandelstam. This was a further bond between us. He and Theresa married and had four children. I met them at a party and one of their sons was the handsomest young man I have ever seen. He had inherited the good looks of both his parents. Sadly, Michael got involved with a Greek girl and left Theresa. When the divorce came through, he married the Greek girl and went to live in Volos for half the year returning to Canterbury for the other half. Theresa later married another member of the English staff, Michael Irwin, after he had become a widower.

I have already mentioned Kate McCluskey, who had been a student of mine in Glasgow. She became a Shakespeare specialist at Kent. Another Shakespeare scholar joined us from Oxford, Professor Molly Mahood. She became the head of department after Professor Foakes stepped down. She was a devout Christian, but I heard she had lost her faith after retirement. An extremely kind woman she always bought Christmas presents for our children. However, she did once disconcert me by criticizing my habit of walking about casually as I was delivering a lecture, a habit I had picked up from Frank Cioffi's laid back style. She was also interested in colonial literature. Professor Louis James, who had taught in Jamaica, came to teach a course in Afro-Caribbean literature. He and his wife Jill became great friends. Three other members of the department who became very close to me were Keith Carabine, Michael Irwin and David Ellis. Keith was a real lad from the North. Along with Stuart Hutchinson, he specialized in American literature. Here the novelist William Faulkner was his primary interest. He was also greatly fascinated by Joseph Conrad that remarkable Pole who entered our merchant navy and elected to write in English. He organized a Conrad conference at Kent at which I gave a paper on Conrad and Schopenhauer. I taught a course on English and Russian fiction with him which involved, among other things, a comparison and contrast between Conrad's *Under Western Eyes* and Dostoevsky's *The Devils*. Both novels deal with conspirators in an ironic way, but the political contrast between Conrad's lack of illusion and Dostoevsky's commitment to a religious Slavophilism with its view that Russia is the God bearing people to a godless and corrupt West could not be greater. He was kind enough to name his son Edward after me. Michael Irwin was married to a beautiful girl named Stella. She had been a child in Majorca and had close connections with the household of the poet Robert Graves's second wife Beryl. She had been, of course, too young to be one of the poet's numerous 'muses' a habit of his which must have been extremely annoying to Beryl even though they were all 'loves at a distance'. Robert Graves was later to give the T.S. Eliot Memorial lectures at the University.

When Michael Irwin became board chairman, he and Stella always gave a wine and cheese party around Christmas to the English department and other friends which was always a delightful occasion. Michael had a flat in Edinburgh and always attended the 'Fringe' festival there. He was also a talented novelist. He was deeply interested in Thomas Hardy and always went to the annual Hardy conference in Dorchester. He kindly gave me helpful comments on the poems I had written and sent to him.

I should mention David Ellis and his beautiful French wife Genevieve. Genevieve came from Annecy and Barbara and I visited them there when we were on holiday. David asked me to keep the minutes at the board meetings when he became secretary. He had been a pupil of F.R.Leavis whom he greatly admired. He had also been r taught by Leavis's wife Queenie. He thought she detested her male students and was not a good teacher. He wrote a book on Leavis. David's work shows a formidable intellect and I treasure the Saturday afternoons when he and I went round to Cioffi's fine old terrace house for discussions with him. Of course we sometimes amused Frank by our philosophical naivety, but we were learning all the time. The duplicities of Freud were often a topic. Frank also tried to explain the difficulties of Wittgenstein's philosophy. After all he himself had been puzzled when Anscombe had given him sheets of her translation of *Philosophical Investigations* to read in the 1950's. David had a sharp intellect. He had a deep interest in biography. First he wrote a brief book on Wordsworth and later a huge volume on D.H.Lawrence which was the third volume of the Life which he had produced along with John Worthen and Mark Kinkead- Weekes. It covered Lawrence's last years. He produced an excellent study of the nature of biography *Literary Lives* (2000) and more biographical work on Shelley and Byron. He also wrote two books on the problems faced by anyone who tries to write a book on Shakespeare because of the lack of sources. I often look up to the shelves at his twelve volumes and blush at my one book and pamphlet. His great friend and fellow pupil of Leavis, Howard Mills, taught at Kent for some years, but then took up a post at the University of Colorado, living as a solitary with the bears in the mountains. We had thought for some time he might marry Judith Hattaway after her husband Michael Hattaway left her. He was one of our Shakespeare specialists and went to a Professorship at the University of Sheffield. Judith, who lived out at Chartham, was a great friend of ours.

Other members of the department were Martin Scofield and his wife Lynn Innes. Martin brought out three interesting books of the American short story, on various writers' appropriation of the character of Hamlet and on T.S.Eliot. Lynn was particularly interested in colonial literature. We were also lucky to have the well-known novelist Abdul Razak-Gurnah who was board chairman for a period and the New Zealander Rod Edmond who also had a spell as board chairman, the post I had managed to avoid. I taught at Kent from 1966 to 1992 when I took early retirement on favourable terms during the Thatcher period. Towards the close I had a spell teaching in Germany at the famous University of Jena which I will describe later. After retirement I was made an Honorary Research Fellow of the School of English.

Over the years things changed greatly in both the social and academic structure at Kent. It soon became clear that the modern languages teachers felt that the students did not have sufficient time to cope with a foreign tongue in the four terms of part two. They wanted the full three years from the start. So the faculty moved from a four year to a three year dear and the interdisciplinary 'Britain and the Contemporary World' was scrapped. As I have already said the Oxford-like college system with its masters and moral tutors disappeared. English abandoned compulsory courses and became a matter of options. It took on as much more ideological tinge. Creative writing was introduced and its staff eventually came to outnumber the department staff. I very occasionally gave one of its evening readings and, as I looked at the forty or so girls sitting in front of me, I thought to myself: 'Poor deluded souls, you all think you are going to win the Booker prize'. Still, as Byron said: 'The best of life is but intoxication' and it was intoxication to which they had succumbed.

20 FAMILY LIFE

We had returned from New Zealand with two lovely children, Matthew and baby Edward. Both were the delight of their grandmother and of my sister Edith who greatly enjoyed the times we visited them in their bungalow in Shavington. This was a village near Newcastle-under-Lyme where my sister worked in the Girls' High School as a teacher of economics. Barbara's father and mother also delighted in them, particularly Grandpa Watts who was greatly amused when Matthew, imitating my mockery of the FBI films we used to watch in California, used to run into the room with a toy gun crying 'This is the FBI, drop your pants'.

Our marriage was a very happy one with many journeys to France Germany and Italy. French literature deeply interested both of us as it was later to engross Edward. I was particularly interested In Tolstoy and had written a book on him. But more and more I grew fascinated with Germany, a country whose beautiful landscapes were then not well known. In particular we loved Thuringia with its beautiful forests and its towns Naumburg, Jena and Weimar. We had two good friends in Jena, Jochen and Gudrun Sander. Jochen taught English literature at the university where I had had a spell of two weeks as a visiting lecturer in 1988, a year before the Russians left. In so far as we saw them at all the Russians seemed thoroughly demoralized. The next year was of course, to see the end of the yoke of communism when the Berlin wall came down. More and more I grew to admire the questioning mind of Friedrich Nietzsche who had grown up in Naumburg and attended the famous school of Schulpforta on the outskirts of the town.

Sometimes we stayed in that capital of sex, Paris. Barbara, who was very mature in such matters, said to me: 'I don't care what you get up to so long as you don't tell me about it'. She had forgiven my dalliance with the student in Buffalo and with a beautiful Jewish graduate student at Kent. All the American graduate students at Kent were sad and angry at the shootings of students protesting against the war in Vietnam at Kent State University back home which occurred at that time.

When first coming to Canterbury we had rented a terraced house in a block the council had made available to accommodate the influx of university teachers. We made many friends there from departments other than English, including teachers from History, French, Economics and Physics. But we soon moved to a larger semi- detached house in St Stephen's Green which, after some delay because of an acute shortage of bricks at the time, had been designed and built by an excellent local builder Mr Gawler. Having read the poem El Balcon by the Spanish poet Jorge Guillen I had asked him to put a balcony on the front. From that balcony one could see a splendid view across Beverley Meadow to the cathedral tower and pinnacles, a view which was to inspire several poems. During the war the old house next to us had been a farm with the cowsheds where our houses now stood. A local once told us that during the war he had seen a German plane flying low over the meadow towards the farm. On the right of the field in a copse ran a disused railway embankment which was called the Crab and Winkle Line because it had connected Canterbury with the fishing town of Whitstable.

Our two boys were very different, physically and mentally. Matthew, the elder, had had to have an eye operation in Glasgow to correct a squint. He also had slight scoliosis or curvature of the spine and was prone to asthma. We felt this made learning to read difficult for him, though later he was to became a passionate reader of the crime novels of Agatha Christie. Very early on he developed an obsession with toy cars. Later on he was to go to work in a garage in Birmingham after having tried various jobs locally, including working on a farm and as a baggage loader at Manston Airport. He was determined to earn his own living and make his own way, even though this meant a somewhat lonely life for several years in the dismal town of Brierley Hill whose only advantage was being near the beautiful Bewdley on the Severn. Edward, on the contrary, was robust from the start and was reading by the age of four before he went to the infant school across the road. There he pleased all his teachers. He was to sail through all exams and was supremely happy, but, as I shall later recount, his life ended 'in shallows and in misery'.

Early on after our settling in Canterbury, my wife Barbara had a family tragedy. Her brother Dennis was very clever and in these days would certainly have gone to university, but as was the case earlier with my sister Edith, going to university was a rare privilege at the time. He became a magistrate's clerk in his hometown of Slough. He was highly regarded by the lay bench and was studying to get further qualifications at night school. He had married a beautiful girl called Margaret who astonished us all because her parents the Lawrences were both so deadly dull. Though not musically sophisticated she had a beautiful soprano voice. She had a sister called Pamela. After she had had two healthy sons, Gregory and Malcolm, she developed cancer and died in her early thirties.

A short while after Dennis was offered the post of chief clerk to the magistrates in Kendal near the Lake District. No sooner had he unpacked his things than he died of a heart attack. This left us with the problem as to who was going to look after the two young boys. Gregory was about the age when pupils do the eleven plus exam and Malcolm was three. In a sense there might have been no problem for Barbara and me, for Margaret's sister Pamela had given her a solemn promise that she would look after the children if something happened to Margaret. But we were in for a surprise.

I have now to narrate an episode whish shows human nature at its most base and repellent. No sooner had Margaret's death occurred than her sister wrote a letter to Barbara saying that she would have nothing to do with the two boys and that we were not to trouble her about them. This posed a dilemma. As we already had two sons Barbara and I felt we could not take on both boys Barbara's mother Ella had long been widowed and was now getting on in years. Nevertheless she felt able to take on the younger child at least for the foreseeable future. We would take Gregory. During the holidays however we would all seven stay in our house which meant, of course, quite a Christmas gathering for Barbara to deal with. We had to have a loft extension as we were short of bedroom space. The view towards the cathedral across the meadow from the loft window of the front bedroom was of course s splendid one.

The evil side of human nature was further confirmed when we received a phone call from the husband of Margaret's sister Pamela saying that he had consulted a solicitor and that the solicitor would take proceedings against us if we raised the question of his wife's promise to her sister about the two boys. It was as though we were living in one of the more sombre novels of Charles Dickens.

For now we coped. We treated the orphaned boys as if they were members of our own family. Barbara went to see the headmaster of the local grammar school in Canterbury, the Simon Langton, to get Gregory into the school even though his eleven plus result had been borderline. She was successful and he had a happy time at school where his manual skills were put to good use when it came to constructing scenery and managing the lighting for the school plays. Gregory's father Dennis had been something of a handyman.

It soon became evident that Barbara's mother was getting too old to look after the younger boy Malcolm. She had long attended a nonconformist church in Slough however and there she met a young couple who could not have children. They took to Malcolm and adopted him and gave him a happy family life. He did well at school and university and eventually started a business of his own. Sadly his adoptive mother died of cancer when she was quite young.

21 MEETING MRS MANDELSTAM

By E. B. Greenwood

Note: an abridged version of this was published in *The New Criterion* for February 2021

I

I visited Nadezhda Mandelstam at her Moscow flat in August 1975. I had struggled with her husband's difficult poetry in Russian with the aid of various translations, mistranslations and cribs, and such articles as I could find, for a number of years. The most rewarding aids to understanding it were, in fact, her own magnificent autobiographical studies *Hope Against Hope* and *Hope Abandoned*, each of which I had read as soon as it became available in translation. Her husband's character and destiny as man and poet are, as she herself was to emphasize to me when I eventually met her, the thematic centre of each work. But there was still more to her own works than that. I felt that they continued into an unpropitious and iron age that gift for the imaginative recreation of the physiognomy of both life's external forms and its inner spirit which the great Russian memoir writers of the nineteenth century, Aksakov, Herzen and Kropotkin had achieved. However, whereas her husband's poetry, apart from the perspicuous and, in retrospect, prophetic ode of May 1918

Proslavim, bratia, sumerki svobody

Let us glorify, brothers, the twilight of freedom

partook of that obliquity of approach characteristic of what Ortega Y Gasset called 'the dehumanization of art' (for all that Mandelstam's obliquities had their roots in centrally human themes) her own work had a nineteenth century explicitness and fullness of content and form.

When, therefore, I planned to join a school trip with ten boys and their Russian teacher as co-driver across Belgium, Germany, Poland and White Russia to camp in Minsk, Smolensk, Moscow and Leningrad (as it then still was) one of my keenest hopes was that of visiting a person with whom I seemed to have relived much that was momentous in both her and her husband's past. I made enquiries of a friend who had visited Mrs Mandelstam so that I could find out her address before I left, but they, unfortunately, were in the Far East, and I had to set off without it. I did discover, however, that she had a fondness for gin and that this, apparently, was not readily available to the ordinary Russian. I, therefore, bought a bottle of gin before setting off and duly preserved it intact during a long and dusty journey in a crowded van.

However the principle object of my journey to Russia was to see Tolstoy's house at Yasnaya Polyana, the place without which, he once said, he could not conceive of life, a sentiment I was to discover was aptly displayed on a notice there when I eventually reached the place. Yasnaya Polyana is about a hundred or so miles south of Moscow, near the provincial town of Tula, and Intourist visitors were then technically supposed to have a visa in order to visit it. My friend had made many efforts to obtain such a visa before our departure, but as our route to Moscow was the Minsk Smolensk one and so, unlike the entry route from the south, did not pass near Tula, he was told that it was impossible to get such a document in advance and that I should go to the Intourist office when we reached Moscow. On crossing the frontier at Brest Litovsk, a name no reader of Russian history can see without a shock of recognition, we were surprised to be greeted by a girl who told us that she was to be our guide. As there were twelve of us in the minibus it seemed that we were technically a party, and every party has to have a guide to accompany them along their route. Even though there were only twelve places in the bus, room would have to be made.

Room accordingly was made and as we now had a representative of Intourist on board the possibility of my visiting Yasnaya Polyana was broached almost at once. It was a three day or so journey to Moscow and the question of my trip to Yasnaya Polyana was trotted out for an airing each day. Almost as soon as we reached Moscow, I went with the guide to the famous (or infamous) Intourist office in Gorky Street. It was on a Friday and it soon emerged that the question of a journey to Yasnaya Polyana was not going to be a simple one. Why, for example, had I not obtained a visa for the visit in London? It was impossible to get to Yasnaya Polyana by train and slotting me in on a coach trip was also, for some mysterious reason, out of the question. Looking back on it I suppose that was because it might have meant some ordinary Russians meeting a Westerner. If I wished to go I should have to have a private car with a chauffeur and a guide and the cost for the day trip would be around forty pounds. I must come to the office on the Monday morning with our accompanying guide to finalise the arrangements and there was no guarantee in the meantime that even these arrangements would be possible. Consequently I must spend the weekend in suspense about the visit that, as I had been at pains to point out, was the main purpose of my long journey to Russia.

I duly met the guide at 9-0 o'clock on Monday at the Intourist office. It turned out that her Friday inquiries had led her to assume my trip to Yasnaya Polyana would be the next day, when the rest of the party was leaving, stopping overnight at Novgorod. She had, therefore, already made a booking on the *Krasnaya Strela* (Red Arrow) the midnight train from Moscow to Leningrad (what reverberations for the reader of *Anna Karenina*) for the next day, Tuesday. When, however, we presented ourselves at the excursion bureau to finalize my trip for the next day, we were told much to the guide's surprise and chagrin that this was impossible because Yasnaya Polyana was closed on Tuesdays. This, it appeared, was not what my guide had been led to believe before the weekend. However Wednesday was all right, so after arranging the excursion for that day we hurried over to the bureau at the Metropole hotel in order to get my train ticket changed from Tuesday to Wednesday. The documentation for this could not be effected immediately, and as Soviet Russia was a land where small pieces of paper were exceedingly important, I had to arrange to meet my guide at the Metropole again that afternoon. There, after another hour's dashing about from bureau to bureau, she at last obtained the ticket.

All this had a material bearing on my visit to Nadezhda Mandelstam, for my being unable to go to Yasnaya Polyana on the next day meant that I would have a whole day in Moscow to myself when the rest of the party had gone. What had hitherto been a faint hope growing fainter as various excursions with the others had pleasantly consumed my time in Moscow, now suddenly loomed not merely as a very real possibility, but even as a duty. It seemed I would not have to dispose of that bottle of gin myself after all. There was only one obstacle now. I did not know Mrs Mandelstam's address or telephone number. I certainly did not feel I should ask the Intourist guide about this in case it both embarrassed her and got Mrs Mandelstam into trouble. The two volumes of her memoirs were, of course, not even allowed into the Soviet Union. Even the Soviet edition of her husband's poems which I was carrying had been quizzically scrutinized at the border. It was clear that they were trying to prevent both Bibles and any of the recent works of Solzhenitsyn getting into the Soviet Union. Some way or other I should have to solve the problem of getting to see Mrs Mandelstam. The weather had turned colder and more uncertain when we had entered Russia. Indeed at Brest Litovsk we had met our first rain for some time and thunderstorms had been hovering around the Moscow region. However the next day was a perfect summer day. I saw the rest of the party off to Novgorod in the minibus under a clear sky. As the run rose still higher it grew warmer, but not oppressively hot as the city can be in August. Here was I alone with the whole day at my disposal to spend as I wished. I really *must* see Mrs Mandelstam somehow. Surely I could get her telephone number from somewhere.

    I had been told that in addition to our embassy we had a cultural attaché in an office somewhere off Kutuzovsky Prospekt not far from the Ukraine hotel. Clutching my bottle of gin, I set off there by bus. I reached the office shortly after nine, but was stopped by a militia man at the entrance. I realized that in these days of hold ups and kidnaps he had the perfectly legitimate wish to establish my nationality and identity, and, as soon as I displayed my passport, he let me in.

There were two secretary- telephonists behind the desk and not liking to reveal my errand immediately, I mumbled some question as to whether they had a reading room. There were one or two little side rooms for consultation (probably for businessmen) but there was no reading room as such. I then asked about the possibility of finding a private telephone number and address. At this moment a man appeared with a briefcase in his hand. The girl directed me to him. I was not altogether surprised that he did not seem to have heard of Mandelstam for I had been given to understand that the office was much more concerned with business matters than with cultural ones (despite its name) and my first impressions had confirmed this. When I inquired about obtaining a private phone number I was told that no public directories of private subscribers were available. I expressed some surprise at such a state of affairs, and it was intimated to me that the revolution could have had something to do with it. The Russian secretary-telephonist might have been able to help me, but she was away on holiday and they only had a 'temporary' from England who did not speak any Russian. I concealed my amazement at the situation of not having a girl who could speak Russian in such an office. I could not help thinking of the presumably scores of girls studying Russian who would snatch at the chance of such a job in Moscow. It was obvious I was not going to get anywhere and the man from whom I was making my inquiries had intimated that he had an important meeting at the Embassy itself in a few moments. It seemed from what he said that there would be no one at the Embassy who would be able to help with my problem either. I thanked him and left, having decided to walk to the Kievskaya station just round the corner and take the metro into the city centre.

As I turned right from Kutuzovsky Prospekt and walked along a pleasant street lined with trees here and there, I passed a building with the notice *Soiuz Sovetskikh Pisatelei* (Union Of Soviet Writers) on a plaque beside the door. It was a long shot and perhaps risky in some ill-defined sort of way but surely I must try and see if, as seemed likely, there was someone willing and able to help me there. It was half past nine. I rang the bell. A lady who seemed to be a cleaner appeared and I tried to explain my errand in none too fluent Russian. She was very understanding and said that one of the staff would be arriving soon. Sure enough a man with a briefcase appeared. I followed him into the office explaining who I was and what was the nature of my problem. For the first time I mentioned the name Mandelstam and I watched his face to see if it betrayed any reaction. There was not the least flicker of recognition that the name was any different from Kuznetsov or Popovich or any other name. He took from a drawer a list of the members of the Writers Union. Now I knew that the name of a man who had died in one of Stalin's camps in 1938 would not be in a directory of current writers and I very much doubted if his widow's name would be there, considering that her famous memoirs were not allowed into the country. What surprised me was that the man's whole bearing and helpful demeanour suggested that he had simply not heard of either the poet or his widow, unless, of course, he was bluffing. After I had been unsuccessful, as I expected, he suggested that I should return at noon when the English-speaking foreign editor would be there. I then thanked him and left.

I travelled into the city centre. It was a delightful summer day with people in blouses and summer jackets all around. I noticed a line of telephone booths.

I entered a vacant booth and looked to see if there was a number for directory inquiries displayed. There were, of course, no telephone books. I couldn't find one. Eventually I asked a lady just leaving a booth how I could find a private number. She did not mention anything about directory enquiries, but indicated a *spravochnik* or information booth just across the square. I joined the queue there and, when I reached the window, I asked if they had such a thing as a list of private telephone subscribers. No, she had no such list, but she could give me a number to ring for directory inquiries. I noted the number and went back to the telephone booth. I cannot remember for certain, but I think I then noticed that the number she had given me was in fact displayed somewhere near the telephone. I rang it, but it was engaged. I tried again three or four times after suitable intervals. Always engaged! I walked in the park by the Kremlin wall, carrying the by now somewhat irksome bottle of gin in my bag. I ate an ice cream. Then I tried again in another booth. Still engaged! Time was getting on. Noon was approaching. I must get the metro back to the Union Of Soviet Writers.

I travelled back to the Kievskaya station and then started to Union office. I had almost reached the door when I suddenly noticed a couple of phone booths against a nearby building. Why not have one more go? I entered a booth, dialled the number for inquiries and, to my utter and now slightly disconcerted amazement, got through. Now began a sort of nightmare. I explained as best as I could my predicament; how I only had a name and no address and wished to find a number. What was the name? I gave it. Could I repeat it? I did so. Surely there was nothing so terribly recondite about such a name. I felt it should be no more formidable to a Russian telephone operator than say the name 'Wilkinson' pronounced with a foreign accent would be to an English telephone operator. Could I spell the name *bukva iz bukvy*, letter by letter? Unfortunately I had never really mastered the Russian names of the letters of the alphabet. However I spelled out the name as best I could. I had to repeat it four times. Meanwhile the sun was beating through the windows of the booth and I was getting more and more sweaty and more and more uneasy. The operator had not yet said she would give me the number and I suspected she was consulting with some superior as to whether my call should be allowed through. I was worried too in case my whole enterprise might get Mrs Mandelstam into trouble. Later when I got back to England and discussed the whole matter with a teacher of Russian I discovered that I had been stressing the name Mandelstam on the first syllable when I should have been stressing it on the last. Now stress is extremely important in Russian, but I still wonder whether such delay as occurred could be accounted for by a slip like that. Then suddenly the operator gave me a number. I jotted it down with some difficulty in my pocket dictionary as my biro had started to dry up in the heat. At last there it was on the page. The only question now was whether it was the right Mandelstam.

I dialled it. A frail voice answered and almost immediately I recognized that I had the right person. I could hardly believe that I was talking to the very same person I knew from the books, the person who had experienced and suffered so much. It was like a dream. I heard myself, so to speak, explain the situation to her in a way that one hears oneself speak as a third person in dreams. 'Yes, come to me, come now, come at once.' I knew Mrs Mandelstam had taught English, but somehow I felt that I must try to simplify my speech over the phone in order to make it as clear as possible. I asked for her address. It seemed a particularly long and difficult Russian name for me to catch. It was the operator's situation in reverse. I did not have to ask her to repeat it letter by letter, however, only syllable by syllable. I had a moment of panic though when I couldn't get the biro to write on the fly leaf of my dictionary and I thought it had dried up for good. Sweat was rolling down my face. I pressed down on the page. To my relief the point made a mark. I had to request more repetition, but at last I got the whole thing down in reasonably legible form and repeated it. We talked a little more. Mrs Mandelstam sounded suspicious. 'You talk foreigner's English' she said. I did not want to insult her by saying that I was deliberately trying to simplify my speech. I could understand that she might be worried that I was some kind of investigator trying to compromise her. I explained that I was a teacher of English literature with an interest in Russian literature. Inwardly I cursed the fact that I had made an appointment at the Union of Soviet Writers. The appointment was now superfluous as I had Mrs Mandelstam's telephone number and address, but I felt it would be discourteous of me not to keep it. Keeping it, however, would delay me and I was very struck, and in a strange way moved, by Mrs Mandelstam's insistence that I should come to her at once, without delay. At the same time I felt I couldn't explain the reason for the delay and I was worried that if I said I had mentioned her name at the Union Of Soviet Writers it would be a reason for anxiety on her part. I said by way of excuse that I was a fair distance from her as far as I could understand, for I was near the Kievskaya metro station, but I added that I would try and get a taxi and would be with her as soon as possible.

I re-entered the Union of Soviet Writers with a sinking feeling. I was worried about bringing up the name of Mandelstam again and disquieted by the delay my calling there might impose on me. I was obviously remembered from earlier and was not taken into the same office as before, but whisked along the road a couple of blocks and ushered into the office of the foreign editor. Here, to my surprise, I found two fairly elderly and quite benign ladies. They never asked me about my earlier request, about which they did not seem to have been informed. It looked as though they thought I was merely a visiting English writer, a translator of Russian poetry, perhaps, who wished to pay his respects at the shrine of the Union Of Soviet Writers. In a way this was a godsend. I would not have to repeat the original purpose of my visit and thus possible embarrassment all round could be avoided. At the same time I could not just leave. I would have to make conversation for a while. I might even be invited for lunch. I chafed inwardly at the delay, but smiled politely and genuinely admired the good English of my interlocutors.

What Russian poetry had I translated? As a matter of fact I had translated Blok's *The Twelve* into English verse, both for my own pleasure and for use in a university course on the Russian revolution. I mentioned this while admitting at the same time that none of my translations had been published. A number of English translators of Russian poetry and prose for their English language periodical Soviet Literature (had I heard of it?) were mentioned. Three of them, it seemed lived in Moscow. Did I know any of them? I shifted uncomfortably, wondering what sort of people these compatriots of mine, who had bravely put down roots in this to me still somewhat exotic (if outwardly drab) place, could possibly be. Yes, I said, I had heard of the periodical Soviet Literature. I did not actually subscribe and was not sure whether my own university's library did, but I would investigate as soon as I got back. Meanwhile a copy of the current issue was kindly hunted out for me. I felt I must strike out boldly and said that I had recently published *The Comprehensive Vision* a book on Tolstoy. They expressed interest and talked of my sending a copy for possible review in *Soviet Literature*. What Soviet writers did I know? I tried to think of someone appropriate and respectable. I recalled that Marshak had established a reputation in the West as a translator of Burns and I asked about him. A benign, pitying and rather patronising smile appeared on both their faces. Marshak? Didn't I know that Marshak had been dead for ten years. I too smiled at my own folly, and, turning over its pages expressed both admiration and thanks for the copy of Soviet Literature they had given me. I then asked the most vocal of them for her name and the office address and noted them both down with what I felt was an appropriate expression of gratitude. This seemed the moment to start a kind of coda of farewell. After a few more pleasantries I managed to slip away. They had not brought up the question of my original request earlier that morning. Was this tact or simple ignorance on their part? I had only been with them for about twenty minutes. I felt profoundly grateful for both these facts.

Now I must find a taxi. I had already had some slight experience of taxi seeking in Moscow and was not too sanguine. Certainly no taxis seemed to be coming down the street. I walked toward Kutuzovsky Prospekt which went by on a sort of bridge or embankment above. I turned left into a road sloping up towards it and to my surprise and delight I saw about half a dozen taxis in the shadow of the embankment.

Delight was immediately succeeded by disappointment as I saw they were all in various stages of disrepair. A rather tough and aggressive looking man was just appearing from under the bonnet of one of them, formidable spanner in hand. As often happens, the fact that I could see the request which I knew I had to make was bound to draw a blank only spurred me on to make it. It is as though the notion of inevitable failure acts, by some paradoxical process, as kind of comforting stimulus. As I had expected, my inquiries drew a rather gruff response. No, he was *not* available. If I wanted a taxi I must go and queue at the rank along the road. Fortunately, when I reached the top of the slope towards Kutzuzovsky Prospekt the rank did not seem too far ahead. Fifty or so yards before it was a militiaman passing the time of day with rather a pretty girl. Could I get a taxi just ahead?

He pointed to the rank smilingly with his baton and looked at the girl with an expression that seemed to imply their mutual recognition of the madness of foreigners was one more bond between them. I reached the post which marked the taxi stand. A taxi arrived. There was only one other person there and he took it. Fortunately a second taxi soon turned up. When he heard the address I wanted, the taxi driver seemed perfectly happy to take me.

I climbed in and after twenty minutes to half an hour we reached a long road lined with trees with high rise apartments of an identical type on both sides of it. I paid the driver and made my way round the back of the block with the right number. I found an entrance and walked in. Ahead was a fenced in lift, but the number I wanted seemed down a corridor to the left on this, the ground floor. I rang the bell, nervously eying a box for letters against the wall. I heard the rattling of a chain and a face peered out. Immediately I recognized under the wispy white hair an older version of the face I knew from photographs. It was certainly Mrs Mandelstam. She smiled, and, taking off the chain, opened the door wider. She was wearing a nondescript garment. I could not be sure of whether it was a night gown of some kind or an old day dress. Her bony arm was trembling slightly. I could not believe my hope had been realized and my dream had come true. This frail figure had known Akhmatova and Pasternak and 'the terrible years' and I was to be privileged to speak with her.

II

I couldn't really see very clearly what the flat was like and how many rooms it had. There was one off to the left, but that she seemed anxious to keep private. Perhaps it was her bedroom? She ushered me into a narrow and small but well lit room to the right. There was a window at the far end. This seemed to be the kitchen, perhaps the sitting room as well. We sat at a little table. I remember thinking that she was so old and frail that it at least seemed a kindness on someone's part that she had a ground floor flat. I proudly produced my bottle of gin saying I understood that such delights were not easy to come by in the Soviet Union. She smiled and thanked me. I then tried to explain my 'foreigner's English' and told her the whole story of my difficulties in finding her telephone number.

Did no Soviet cities have directories of private numbers I asked, saying that in London all one need do if one wanted a number was to go to a phone booth and look it up in a directory. 'Once we too had such directories' she sighed. Just as previously I had been embarrassed by having to go to the Union Of Soviet

Writers with the name of Mandelstam, so now, amusingly enough, the situation was reversed and I felt ashamed of having come to Mrs Mandelstam with a copy of Soviet Literature on me. I kept it hidden for the moment. But I felt I must tell her how I had tried to find her number if only to see whether I had done anything that might prove compromising to her. I told her about the nature of my trip to the Soviet Union and how I had not liked to mention her to our guide even though the latter seemed quite likeable and pleasant. She seemed glad I had not done so. 'Don't trust these pleasant girls,' she said, 'for all their charm they are all members of the KGB.' I felt this might be a pardonable exaggeration. 'Perhaps they all used to be,' I said 'but there are so many more visitors to the Soviet Union now that I am sure they have to co-opt girls who are outside the KGB.' 'Oh yes, they are all pretty and charming these Sonyas and Tanyas,' she continued, but don't trust them an inch, they are all good party members set to spy on visitors.'

I explained about asking directory inquiries for her number and was relieved to see she did not seem to be worried about that. I then mentioned my visit to the Union Of Soviet Writers and was still more relieved to see that she was ironically amused by it rather than disquieted. 'Oh no one would know me there,' she said decisively, as though she took a quiet pride in the fact. She even turned over a page or two of my copy of Soviet Literature with a sort of benign amusement. I explained my situation as a teacher of English literature and stumblingly tried to express something of my admiration for her books. To my utter amazement she said she would like to have a copy of her book. I was taken aback. It could be that, though she very likely had a manuscript, she had not been able to get hold of a printed copy of her own book. After all it was not allowed into the country. 'What a pity,' I said, 'the first volume is now out even in paperback in the West and I could easily have brought one if I had known you hadn't one, but, of course, I didn't even know I was going to succeed in getting to see you.' 'Oh, I meant a copy of the work in Russian, not a translation' she replied. I realized how stupid of me it had been to suppose otherwise. Oddly enough I was to see a copy in Russian (where it was simply entitled *Memuary, (Memoirs)* for the first time in a bookshop in Stockholm on our way home. That Swedish bookshop had a far wider selection of both pre- and post-revolutionary Russian literature than any I saw in the Soviet Union. I had even heard a woman in *Dom Knig* (The House of Books) ask for Pushkin only to be told that they hadn't a copy. We talked a little further about her two volumes of memoirs and it was then that she told me that her husband was the real centre of her works. I respectfully questioned this to some degree, saying that though Mandelstam was certainly at their centre, they nevertheless dealt with many other persons, in particular with Akhmatova and with the Formalists. I asked her about the Formalist critic Viktor Shklovsky. She said that when he divorced and married a much younger woman she had had to choose between his previous wife Vasilissa and him. Apparently she had chosen Vasilissa.

She told me that Akhmatova had been very afraid, almost paralysed with fear. I asked her about Akhmatova's poetry. Did she like the early love poetry? Not really. There was too much of the great 'elegant' lady, about her ego and its sufferings, a kind of enjoyment of the unhappy role of refined heroine, a constant note of self-regard. To my surprise (if I understood her correctly) even *Requiem,* the poem about the purges, did not receive the highest kind of praise. No, Akhmatova's best poems had never been published, except for a few lines that Lydia Chukovskaya had printed. Chukovskaya, by the way, was writing a book against her (I presumed against Mrs Mandelstam herself). There was obviously some kind of in fighting here which I could not fathom. Those fine poems which Akhmatova had been too fearful to publish, or even, perhaps, to circulate very widely, were all political poems in that they were about the sufferings under the Terror.

Mrs Mandelstam quoted four lines of them from memory as better than anything in the lyrics of the young Akhmatova. Unfortunately my Russian was not good enough to grasp the sense of an oral rendering, and I foolishly did not ask her to repeat them so that I could write them down. I showed Mrs Mandelstam the Soviet edition of her husband's poems. 'That is a horrible book, I don't wish to know about it. The editor (Khardjiev) is a scoundrel. He printed inferior texts deliberately. It is horrible, horrible.'

Mrs Mandelstam then asked me to do one or two things for her in the West. This necessitated writing down addresses. When she saw me writing down on the fly leaf of the Soviet edition of her husband's poems she said they would be sure to look at the book as I was leaving and, noting an address on it, would confiscate it. Not for the first time I noticed an element of nervousness, not to say paranoia in her. 'No, they won't confiscate it,' I said 'or even see it, for I'll tear the page out and hide it in my wallet.' She was for the most part unwilling to mention by name people in the West with whom she had contact, except, of course, those she had to mention as part of her request. She spoke of an Oxford professor (whom she would not name) who had invited her abroad for a visit, but she would not leave, she said, because she was sure that once she had got outside the country, they would not let her back in. 'I hate this country, but whether it is the language, or my husband's poetry in that language, whatever it is, I just could not bear not to be allowed back her, here is the place I wish to die.' I keenly felt her fear of what Shakespeare called 'the bitter bread of banishment.'

I asked her if she was much troubled now by the authorities. Surely they did not persecute her now she was getting old. What harm could she do them? She said she was still worried. It seemed that while she was at the dacha of some friends, her apartment had been broken into and the KGB had used this affair as an occasion to suggest that she was somehow implicated in the theft of things to be smuggled to the West. She still feared the Lubyanka prison and interrogation as a very real possibility. Horrible too was the fact that some visitors from the West whom she had trusted had stolen from her a rather precious copy of Pushkin in order, she thought, to demonstrate to friends in the West that they had really been with her. I saw why apparent incoherences in some of her stories and why paranoiac fear, and, for that matter, a not entirely dissipated distrust of myself, might well be warranted. At any rate, it seemed I was not to see any more of the flat, but was to stay at the kitchen table for the whole of our conversation. That seemed quite privilege enough in the presence of such a person. In fact the kitchen was probably the whole of the flat!

She told me that she had not been out of the Soviet Union for fifty years, though before the age of sixteen she had journeyed to the capitals of Europe. She spoke scathingly of Soviet writers and of the country under the regime, saying it was full of discontent, inefficiency and drunkenness. I gently ventured to hint on my knowledge of Tolstoy's 'The Devil Was The First Distiller' and of Dostoevsky's work that drunkenness had not been unknown in Russia before the revolution, but she insisted that the drunkenness which concerned her was a post-revolutionary phenomenon. I mentioned that I was going to go to Leningrad. 'It is a dead city, a dead city' she said. I remember how even before the revolution, in 1916 in fact, her husband had seen it as Petropolis, a sort of stone city of the dead when he wrote:

V Petropole prozrachnom my umrem

We shall die in transparent Petropolis.

I reflected that Mrs Mandelstam might well be thinking of the poetic image he had stamped on her mind, and not of the real place, which she had perhaps not seen for years. When I said I was going to Yasnaya Polyana the next day to see Tolstoy's home, a twinkle appeared in her eyes and she said: 'Look at all the peasants in the village. They all look like Leo Tolstoy.' It suddenly occurred to me that this was probably a joke she had heard as a girl when it was going the rounds in pre-revolutionary St Petersburg.

We talked of Tolstoy and Dostoevsky and it emerged that just as every thinking person is a Platonist or an Aristotelean, so too everyone is a Tolstoyan or a Dostoevskyan. When I spoke of my book on Tolstoy she expressed her wish that I had brought a copy. I wished I had. Not that I would have expected her to read it, with her memories and burden of sad experience to reflect on. Simply the thought that she had it in her possession would have been recompense enough. I spoke of my great admiration for *Anna Karenina*. She came out with an objection to the truth of the work which struck me on account of its utter idiosyncrasy. She told me that she had been talking with a relative of her friend Galina Von Meck (perhaps even her mother, I don't remember) and this relative had said that in the society of her youth (presumably near contemporary with that of the novel) a woman like Anna would not have been ostracised in the way that Tolstoy portrayed her as being. Perhaps this person had forgotten that even Karenin is prepared to tolerate a discreet affair, it is Anna's bold indiscretion which leads to disaster. After that Mrs Mandelstam, it seemed, had never been able to read the novel without feeling a note of falsity and strain. Even if this objection were correct, it struck me how much of the novel (Levin's perplexities about religion, about the peasantry, and his sometimes fraught relationships with his brother Nicolas, half-brother Koznyshev, and his wife Kitty) would remain unaffected. In any case it seemed to me that the friend's remark might itself be mistaken, perhaps designed to impress with its knowledge of the ways of 'society.' But it seemed that Tolstoy was not so central to Mrs Mandelstam's moral and literary experience as I had hoped. After all, she had had a great poet, her husband, to engross the foreground of her life and imagination, a poet who had suffered horrors even the would-be martyr Tolstoy would hardly have been able to imagine.

Mrs Mandelstam was very proud of her studies in English. She had submitted a thesis (a dozent's) about the use of the accusative case in Old English. She wondered, though, what her English accent sounded like. Was it strange? Was it Americanized or was it English English. She told me proudly that she knew much Shakespeare by heart. She did not learn things off by heart deliberately. She had simply found that when she familiarized herself with a text she loved she could quote it from memory. I recalled to myself how she had preserved much of her husband's poetry that way during the gloomy years when it was not allowed to be published. Meanwhile she was quoting some rather sad lines from Shakespeare. I did not recognize them and I momentarily misunderstood them until I realized she had mispronounced 'woes' as 'vows.' She said they were to do with the pathetic Prince Arthur in *King John*, an appropriate choice. I wish (as with the Akhmatova lines) I had written them down for I could not find anything that recalled what I vaguely remembered when, on my return, I looked through the play. At the same time I even wondered whether she was testing me by seeing whether I, who claimed to be a lecturer in English literature, could identify them. To compensate for not having been able to do so I quoted by heart from *Hamlet* Marcellus' speech on Christmas.

Some say that ever gainst that season comes
Wherein our Saviour's birth is celebrated
The bird of dawning singeth all night long

Which I had once learned for a school production.

It emerged that the Russian Orthodox faith had become very important to Mrs Mandelstam. Here again the strong reactions of the Christian Akhmatova and of Mandelstam himself against the neo-paganism of the Russian Symbolists and Futurists, so movingly documented in her *Memoirs,* had probably been of decisive influence. I remarked that we had greatly enjoyed the singing at Smolensk cathedral and had been very impressed by the youthfulness of the bishop. She replied that so many of the higher clergy were young because their predecessors had been shot. She told me that a young priest she knew who had been critical of the regime in a sermon had been almost killed in a car crash and she was convinced that the whole thing had been rigged so that the 'accident' was nothing less than attempted murder. She herself tried to get to a service each Sunday, but the nearest working church was quite far away and this necessitated a taxi. I asked her what she thought of an orthodox thinker like Shestov, but she conveyed the impression that she had no need of the thoughts of Shestov or even, perhaps, of Berdyaev, on the subject of religion, for when it came to that her own meditations were rich enough.

Indeed she told me that she was writing a third book, not memoirs this time, but a book on orthodox Christianity. I must not mention this to anyone. I wondered to myself whether this turn to Christianity (so evident at times in the *Memoirs* themselves) had been the occasion for Lydia Chukovskaya's writing a book against her. I had no particular reason to. It was just a 'hunch.' After all, Orthodoxy in itself was a protest against the regime. We discussed Solzhenitsyn (who I think she saw as a courageous man but as sometimes clumsily Soviet in his writing), Brodsky, (a nice man, but not as poetically and linguistically gifted as he thought and educated in a linguistically bad environment), Proust (whom she much admired) and the contemporary literary scene (conspicuous for her by its absence) and even politicians (Kosygin was the first whose hands were not stained with blood).

She saw the whole country as running down, industry and agriculture as in a terrible state, shortages and drabness everywhere. She wanted to know if I thought the English had had any literary figure of significance to succeed Eliot. She did not seem to know 'La Figlia Che Piange' (one of my favourite Eliot poems) and I wondered whether this was perhaps absent from her edition as it had been from the old Penguin *Selected Poems*. I asked her about her view of Nabokov. 'A great writer lost to Russia' she said. I certainly agreed with the latter part of her judgment, but couldn't help doubting the former.

She gave me to understand that no mail was allowed to reach her either from inside or outside Russia. We had been talking for about two and a half hours and she seemed tired. I felt I ought to take my leave. It seemed to me that there must be many things I would regret having forgotten to ask her once I had gone, not so much about literary figures, though there would be much there certainly, as about how her immediate neighbours treated her, about the person who had got her the ground floor flat, and what sort of friends she had. Perhaps it is as well I did not explore these matters. I rose to go. We shook hands. She accompanied me to the door. She went up to the post box and opened it. 'See, there is nothing inside' she said 'there never is and there never will be.' The door closed on her farewell smile and I made my way to the tram stop. I had not asked her about Blok as I had meant to, Blok and the nature of poetry on the eve of the First World War, Blok's view of Mayakovsky. That was the first omission that came to mind. I remembered what she had written of Blok in *Hope Abandoned*. Blok had merely imagined the apocalypse, she and her husband had had to live through it. Blok was the better for having died ignorant of the worst that was to come, a worst that, in retrospect, tinges his work with childlike histrionics. I remembered her charity in her memoirs towards Mayakovsky who had adopted, she thought, a cruel braggadocio alien to his sensitive nature. May she be judged as charitably as she judged others, I reflected, though it would seem that her need for our charity in judgment is much less than that of most of us.

NOTE

In a letter dated 10 April 1976, the late Sir Isaiah Berlin wrote to me advising me not to publish this brief memoir at the time, mindful of the way his account of his visit to Anna Akhmatova had led to her persecution by the Soviet authorities. Since then it has been in my files, but friends thought it would be of interest and recall the awful restrictions on human liberty imposed in those dreadful times by a terrible regime. Now in 2023 I wish to add a further note. In !936 Anna Akhmatova wrote the poem 'Voronezh' referring to Osip Mandelastam's exile there. It concluded with the lines

I noch idiot
Kotaraya ne vedaet rassveta.
And the night falls
Which will know no dawn.

For a while under Gorbachev we thought that at last that dawn might be beginning. Subsequent events dashed that hope. Now under Putin's autocracy that night has descended again. I conclude with a poem I recently wrote about this dreadful situation:

Russia Today
Subservient politicians fawn
And generals look on with awe,
As Putin once more show his scorn
For what should be the rule of law.

He surveys war with fearful grin,
Knowing that others count the cost,
His generals tell him he will win
Although they fear that he has lost.

Oh for a Pushkin who admired

The brave Decembrists and their fate,
A Mandelstam whom anger fired
To ridicule the head of state.

Akhmatova who boldly said
How much the foul oppression hurt,
And Pasternak who raised his head
While others groveled in the dirt!

What would they make of Russia now?
Would they not think it much the same?
A place where the subservient bow,
A place of fear and of shame

Where opposition ends in gaol,
Tormented, tortured,, even killed,
The ancient miserable tale,
So Putin's wish can be fulfilled.

22 A VERY SAD EPISODE

My younger son Edward gained a scholarship and entered Wadham College Oxford to read French language and literature. He was at this time a very happy and sociable person, having many friends in Canterbury already, and making many more new ones in Oxford.

Physically he was vigorous and strong, though not interested in games, and mentally he was full of ambition. I have the feeling, however, that his ambition was not to be a scholar, though he excelled in academic work, but to be a great writer. He had indeed applied to Malcolm Bradbury's creative writing course at Norwich, but that was one of his few rejections. The campus novel as practiced by David Lodge and Malcolm Bradbury himself was riding high at the time. Edward was always very interested in girls and Barbara and I had had a scare when we thought he got a local girl, who was only fifteen, pregnant. Fortunately it turned out to be a false alarm. He was to have many affairs, however, both in Canterbury and in Oxford and Barbara called him a 'serial monogamist'.

He sailed through all tests and exams, but perhaps made a bad mistake when after finals, for which he got a starred first, he immediately sat several papers for a research fellowship in French at New College. He had had no respite. I remember our taking him out for a meal to celebrate his finals. He did not enjoy it had some sort of 'turn' and we all had to leave. We should have seen this as a warning sign and insisted that he have a rest before taking another set of hard exams. He was awarded the fellowship, but then made a further mistake by deciding to do his doctoral thesis on one of the most decadent figures of the very decadent French literature of the end of the nineteenth century, Joris Huysmans. Huysmans is best known for his strange novel *La-Bas*, one of the few of his many novels to be translated into English. It is about the very decadent theme of always believing happiness to be elsewhere in a place one cannot reach. Disillusionment is always hovering near. At one point the hero longs to see London at first hand, and then decides it is not worth the bother of going there because simply imagining life in London will give him even greater pleasure. He wrote a novel about a suppurating medieval miracle working female saint from the low countries named Saint Lydwine a subject which could only make an unhealthy mind even more unhealthy. It would hardly be good for someone with precarious mental health to have to produce 100,000 words on such a writer. Edward worked hard on this unhealthy subject, but, as far as writing was concerned, made the fatal mistake of procrastinating. Moreover he spent a year in that dreary uncollegiate, unfriendly though famous institution the *Ecole Normale Superieure* in Paris to enter which he had passed another exam if I remember rightly.

His research fellowship ran out and he failed in his attempt to get a teaching fellowship which might have led to a permanent post and a happy career in Oxford. He had to get a job teaching unresponsive French students English so that he could afford to keep his gloomy Paris flat. Eventually his thesis was completed and he got a doctorate, but by now it was too late and he was becoming seriously mentally ill. This was not helped by his going to a psychiatrist in Paris who plied him with drugs. He had hoped to marry a beautiful young Oxford student of his who came from Birmingham. She did her best to continue to visit him in Paris, but eventually she could face his misery no more and broke off the relationship. Thankfully she later made a happy marriage.

So in the early 1990s Edward came home in a terrible state and remained incapacitated for several years. The psychiatrist he went to in Canterbury also made him go through a gamut of drugs. This was fashionable at the time among many of his helpless and useless profession. Edward had a spell at an offshoot of the Bethlehem hospital in south London. When we visited him there, we were appalled at the feebleness of the treatment on offer. But then mental illness is beyond our present capacities to treat, though some professionals keep pretending it is not.

Edward also had spells of residence in a local mental unit. Here he was given electro-convulsive therapy. He always looked as though he were shell shocked after it, walking with a dazed and vacant expression. Another depressing place for the depressed!

When he came home and used to go out for a walk to town we were in constant fear that he would throw himself in front of a car or under a train. His only respite was when I took him to second-hand bookshops in nearby towns on book buying-expeditions. As this was before online buying had taken over there were still plenty of these. On the way to the bookshop, and while he was browsing, he could look quite elated, but sometimes as I was driving him home I could see his face darken the nearer home we got.

He slept in the front room in the loft. During the day and sometimes at night we would sit at the bottom of the stairs listening to his screaming for hours. If we went up to solace him he would scream and sob and sometimes just beg us to go away as he could not bear to be seen in the state he was in. Whenever he went out we worried that he would never return, having committed suicide. If darkness was approaching, I would anxiously look out of the front door hoping that he would be back before dark. I wrote several poems about this later. So passed the first half of the 1990's.

At length on New Years Eve 1995/1996 the moment we had dreaded arrived. He did not return. Then about noon on January 1 1996 the police came to tell us that his body had been found at the foot of the cliffs at Beachy Head. He had written us a note on the way there apologising for what he was about to do. Later I marvelled at what his state of mind and his resolution must have been as he did that and then took his way to the cliff edge. I tried to get some vain comfort from writing poems about it. We were later to meet a couple who had been walking there and seen him before he took the last decision. The fall they did not see. Barbara could not even bear to look at a photograph of this famous beauty spot and would certainly never visit it.

And now I come to the sad episode of my wife Barbara's death on November 9th 1999 at the age of eighty-six. We had been married for sixty-one years. Barbara had developed a degenerative lung disease called bronchiectasis. From walking to the town together to taking the bus she could now hardly move. She now had respiratory nurses who visited daily to monitor her condition. She also had a charming lady Pauline, who was still quite a beauty in her late fifties, and who visited her daily to wash and dress her and prepare her for bed. She had to have a machine which created oxygen which was then pumped through a pipe to a mask on her mouth. There was one in the downstairs sitting room and one in the bedroom for she had to use the breathing apparatus even when she was sleeping.

My son was working with a car repair firm in Birmingham, but tried to come down to see his mother when he could. Fortunately as her condition rapidly worsened he happened to be with an ambulance and rescue unit at Lyddon in Kent which is close to Canterbury. While still on my own with Barbara I had phoned for an ambulance. The ambulance crew made her comfortable and then left. Her breathing grew stlll fainter and then I was thankful to see Matthew arrive. We decided she would be better in her bed upstairs than in an upright chair. With difficulty we lifted her and carried her up the stairs. As I recall it, she was too inert to put in the chair lift which made our getting her past it more difficult. Later we wondered whether she had died as we were carrying her, for as soon as we had put her in the bed Matthew said that she was not breathing. We called for an ambulance and this time the ambulance crew confirmed that she was dead as soon as they saw her.

Finally I must give thanks and pay tribute to the loving carer, Pauline Burns, who looked after Barbara in her last years of great suffering and who became a great friend.

23 FINAL RECKONING: ON FRIENDSHIP AND FRIENDS

So far I have written this book *Past and Present* on a settee beneath a side window in the upstairs sitting room. My dear Barbara, knowing the academic's predilection for accumulating books, always wanted this room kept clear of books and bookshelves, They were to be confined to the small study beyond the adjoining door. But now the room is full of book shelves, a library in itself. I think though, that, if Barbara were here she would forgive me and encourage my present autobiographical enterprise.

To conclude it I have chosen to write at the small, but lovely antique writing desk we bought long ago at a second-hand shop. Unlike the side window, it has a lovely view over Beverley Meadow to the tower of Canterbury Cathedral so that if I look up from my writing I can gaze at what must be the best urban view in England. On the desk in front of me as I sit there is a row of books by my favourite author and philosopher Friedrich Nietzsche. I mentioned his striking autobiography *Ecce Homo* at the start of this memoir as my model. He would have agreed with me as to the beauty of the mediaeval tower in front of me just as I agree with him that it shelters a faith given over, like all religions, to telling lies which depreciate this earthly life in favour of a fraudulent one. For as Wordsworth beautifully put it in The Prelude this is the one world

Wherein we find out happiness or not at all.

The Greeks whom Nietzsche so admired and taught us so much about life and the world, knew this before they were corrupted by the Platonic Idealism which was to meld with Christianity. I hope the wisdom in the books which line my shelves and the beautiful architecture I look out upon may be aids to reflection.

In the eighteenth-century cricket was played on the meadow, No doubt after it the players would retire for a drink to The Old Beverly pub just over the road. As Omar Khayyam might have said, had he been a Christian: 'Let us make up in the pub for the time we have wasted in the cathedral!' Cricket has always been my favourite sport. It has very complicated rules, like life, but there is one very clear rule which is that when you lose your wicket you are out. In this it is an allegory of life. When your innings is at an end your life is at an end. A perfect allegory! I am 89 as I write this and, again an allegory of the book as life, I hope to reach a hundred pages. At cricket and with a book you can have another innings or write another page, but once your life is over all is at an end. There is no continuation. Full stop!

My life has not been an unusual one. Childhood, boyhood, youth, adulthood, late adulthood, early age, final stage, the seven ages of man of Jacques famous speech in Shakespeare's *As You Like It*.

As I look at the books all round me I hope they may have deposited some wisdom in me to exemplify in this autobiography. We all live in multiple worlds, a public world of history and a more restricted world of family, friends and colleagues. Both Aristotle and Nietzsche rightly saw friendship as one of the most precious things in life. So I must talk about friendship and about some of my friends and their qualities and what they gave me. The first thing to say about friendship is that it is, as the life of Nietzsche shows, precarious. Friends are apt to become estranged, partially, as with Nietzsche and his fellow philologist Erwin Rohde, or wholly, as in the example which I am going to give from my own life. After my Edward's death by suicide, the author A.N.Wilson, whom I had met when he was giving a lecture on Jesus at the University Of Kent, was very sympathetic He invited me to his London club in Pall Mall, The Travellers Club, for lunch, probably the only time I shall penetrate that strange, dominantly male, world. His father had been a manager of Wedgwoods, the pottery firm. Presumably hoping to gentrify him, his father had sent him to a prep school, not realizing that the head master and his wife were both sadistic child abusers. He then 'got' religion and entered a seminary only to find sexual abuse was also rife among the seminarians. Not surprisingly he reacted against the mumbo-jumbo of religion and wrote a violent pamphlet against it. I admire it, but it does not use the deepest argument against it, the one that Nietzsche uses, namely that all religions lie and to join one is the end of intellectual integrity. He concentrates rather on the suffering which religious fanatics inflict on themselves and others. However he later wrote an article in *The Spectator* saying he had become a Christian again.

He seemed to enjoy our lunchtime discussions and learned a lot about philosophy from me for, as he acknowledged, he was not interested in analytic and abstract thought. In the end I think my Nietzschean atheism tired him. Suddenly, without warning, he said he wanted nothing to do with me because I had sent him a poem of mine which poked fun at Alan Bennett. He claimed Alan Bennett was a close friend of his. I think this was a mere pretext and that my atheism was the real reason.

I naturally had many good and helpful friends among my colleagues at the University. These were not confined to the English department. The reason for this was that when the University opened it tried, as many of the other new universities did, to get away from too early specialization in a single subject. In fact it started, as Keele had done, with a four year degree. The first year lasted four terms, in which students had to do a course called 'Britain And The Contemporary World' in which History, Philosophy and European Literature were combined. Students today would envy the fact that students then attended lectures in which there were four members of staff to twelve students. In addition there were formal lectures and tutorials in which students were paired. It was only in their fifth term that students specialized and, even then, they often combined subjects.

In literature my great friends among the teachers were Michael Irwin, David Ellis, Martin Scofield, Henry Claridge, whose charming wife Olga is Ukrainian, Bernard Sharratt whose somewhat convoluted intellect intrigued me and Keith Carabine. I was particularly close to Keith, a fellow Lancastrian. He had a great knowledge of the work of Joseph Conrad and became an editor of the journal *The Conradian*. He also organised a conference on Conrad at the University. We taught jointly a course on English and Russian literature. There could not be a greater contrast between two countries. England, a confident maritime power, Russia, a gigantic land empire which because of this of has been constantly invaded. But because Russia had been invaded from the West so many times, its people became and have remained paranoiac about the West.

This led Russians to develop a strong suspicion of foreign powers and their citizens. Russia was and still is a surveillance society intolerant of dissidents. In particular some of its Slavophil authors developed strong anti -Western feelings which, as we can see, persist today. Here Dostoevsky was particularly guilty. We delighted in teaching his novel *The Devils* and contrasting it with Joseph Conrad's soberly ironic *Under Western Eyes*.

We also enjoyed comparing the psychological insight of George Eliot in *Middlemarch* with that of Tolstoy in what is my favourite novel of all: Tolstoy's *Anna Karenina*. When I taught Conrad in my Thursday morning two hour literary course in The Friends' Meeting House in Canterbury (now the course is online) Keith came along and was a delight to all present. Sadly he is now very ill.

I also enjoyed a good relationship with our first professor of English Reginald Foakes, who was always encouraging and with his successors as heads of the English board Molly Mahood and Peter Stone. Peter, who had been a gifted concert pianist before becoming a university teacher alas dies young.

I must mention my very best student Dan Willis who came to Kent as a mature student. This meant he need only do part two. He came as a mature student, having been given two years leave from his post as head of English in a secondary modern school in Gillingham and his maturity showed. He was a great asset to my course Seventeenth Century Studies which focused on the Civil War period. I tried to introduce students not just to the poets such as Milton and Marvell, but to the philosopher Thomas Hobbes's *Leviathan* and to selections from Clarendon's *History Of The Great Rebellion*. Clarendon's masterpiece is my second favourite work of history after Thucydides' *History Of The Peloponnesian War.*

Both Hobbes and Clarendon greatly admired Thucydides and Hobbes indeed started his literary career by translating him into English. One of the best students in my course was Gavin Esler who later became Chancellor of the University. When Anthony Quinton came to give the Eliot lectures, Quinton chose the topic of conservative thinkers. I think it was Gavin who asked him to put in a word about Clarendon and his great friend Falkland.

But to return to Dan Willis. When he left the university, our close contact did not cease for through him I joined the Thursday literary group I have already mentioned. It had started as part of extra –mural work at the University but when extra-mural teaching started to disappear moved into the town. At least one of its members John Fraser had served in the Second World War in Italy and another, Peter Coulson had been a student at Hertford from 1948 just before I started there. A third Jack Hubbard, who was a very lively discussant, ran a second-hand bookshop in Canterbury. The membership with the next longest membership is Valery Gidlow whose son studied Russian along with my son at the Langton. Her contributions to discussion are highly valuable.

Dan, now in his nineties, has been a stalwart of the group ever since designing its advertising posters and assiduously attends it still. He formatted my privately printed collection of poems *Frozen Leaves* for the printer Mickleprint in 1917.

From colleagues in the history department, I learned much from Ian Jack on the seventeenth century, Maurice Larkin on the materialism and determinism in the French nineteenth century novel (an interesting contrast with George Eliot) Richard

Langhorne on the origins of the First World War and Dick Crampton on Russian history. Dick later got a post at St Edmund's hall Oxford. I was very friendly with Lewis Ryder of the Physics department who was a great admirer of the novels of Dostoevsky. He, David Ellis, Michael Scofield and Bill Bell from the French department often lunched together.

In philosophy I learned much from Richard Norman's lectures particularly his lecture on Nietzsche's *The Genealogy Of Morals* and even more from Sean Sayers. Both were much involved with student protests at the time. These protests were very 'sixties' indeed. The students once blockaded Reginald Foakes's study on the grounds that as a professor he was likely to be a Fascist. He had actually served in the R, A.F. during the war!

Sean held philosophy discussions for those students and staff interested first at the university and then, with the coming of the infectious covid epidemic by zoom He also had convivial drinks when it was possible with the group. I shall be eternally grateful to him for his taking us through Kant's three critiques. No on e in the ancient world doubted that we see such external objects as chairs and tables. Kant, building on the scepticism of Descartes and Hume and the phenomenalism of Bishop Berkeley (thought he always denied unconvincingly in my view that he was a subjective idealist) claimed that we experience only phenomena. Though he rejected all traditional metaphysics he claimed somewhat Platonistically that there are two world the phenomenal world which is the only one we can know and the noumenal world which we cannot know and which, indeed, lies beyond the bounds of what can be said. Unfortunately he then inconsistently went on to do what he had just forbidden because he needed the noumenal world to underpin his to my mind erroneous ethical universalism. Sean was very interested in Marx, but he had an Italian grandfather who was a famous anarchist in America and imprisoned when he returned to Italy during the during the Mussolini period. Sean kindly gave me a translation of a biography of him by Antonio Senta. It was published in English by AK press in 2019.

But by far my greatest friend at Kent and the person who had much the greatest intellectual influence on me was Frank Cioffi. There is an excellent memoir of him by David Ellis. Frank, David and I used to meet every Saturday afternoon for wide ranging philosophical discussions. David has written several biographies and they often discussed the difficulties which face the biographer and the different kinds of biography. The criticism of Freudian psychoanalysis figured prominently in the discussions. Frank had studied Freud, in particular the case histories of which he had a detailed knowledge. He was very contemptuous of such expositors of psychoanalysis as the Philosopher Richard Wollheim. Frank himself came under strong criticism from the Freudians for a spirited broad cast on the BBC in the sixties which was reprinted in The Listener volume 91. The talk had the provocative title 'Was Freud A Liar?' Subsequent work by Frederick Crews who greatly admired Frank, and Malcolm Macmillan in *Freud Evaluated*, Melbourne 1989, in Alan Esterson *Seductive Mirage*, Open Court, 1993 and Richard Webster *Why Freud Was Wrong*, Harper |Collins 1995) and Crew's own book *Unauthorized Freud*, Penguin Books 1998 vindicated Frank. Earlier critics such as the philosophers Ernest Gellner and Adolf Grunbaum had criticized Freud as a pseudo-scientist because of the ways he avoided falsification, but Cioffi's great innovation was to shift the emphasis to Freud as a bad historian because he was an unreliable narrator about his patients as the Wolf Man's own book on Freud's account of him had shown.

Frank was an article man rather than a writer of book length works. But each article had enough concentrated material in it for a book. He always wrote wittily, with a fund of pertinent anecdotes and appositely with no padding. His own essays on Freud were published *In Freud And The question Of Pseudoscience* by Open Court in 1998. In the Preface he acknowledges the stimulus of discussions with David Ellis and myself among others. The book is dedicated to his Indian wife Nalini about whom I will speak later.

Frank's other great interest was the thought of Wittgenstein, not just about philosophy but about anthropology (the Lectures of Fraser's *The Golden Bough*) and critical judgement in aesthetics. Here again his medium was the critical essay. The essays on Wittgenstein were collected in *Wittgenstein On Freud And Frazer*, published by Cambridge University Press in 1998. Again he acknowledges help from discussions with David Ellis and myself. He also included a handsome dedication to myself which ran: 'To Edward Greenwood for three decades of instruction and hilarity.'

Perhaps the most philosophical essay concerns a theme which engaged both of us that of the ultimate loneliness of every human being. It is entitled 'Congenital transcendentalism and the "loneliness which is the truth about things").' The quotation is from section 12 of part 3 of Woolf's novel *To The Lighthouse* where James looking at Mr Ramsay, the character based on Woolf's father the Victorian critic Leslie Stephen, thinks to himself: 'he looked as if he had become physically what was always at the back of both their minds__that loneliness which was for both of them the truth about things.' The essay brings out the width of Frank's reading in literature as well as philosophy. He associates his view with that of Edmund Husserl in *The Paris Lectures* and one of his most cherished quotations that from the Daoist Chuang- Tse who dreamed so often that he was a butterfly that he ends by s wondering 'whether he is a man dreaming that he is a butterfly or a butterfly dreaming that he is a man.'

As Coleridge put it the existence of the I is more certain than the existence of the world the I observes. Tolstoy tells us in *Boyhood* of his looking rapidly to the side 'hoping to catch emptiness unawares where I was not.' Wordsworth too had expressed doubts about the existence of the external world. Wittgenstein too had a strong tendency to solipsism, affirming mysteriously in proposition 5.62 of the *Tractatus* : 'In fact what solipsism *means,* is quite correct, only it cannot be *said*, but shows itself.' He ends this dazzling paper by aligning solipsism with those delusions of reference in which we think some natural phenomenon is speaking to us with some highly important message which we cannot articulate. We find it in Baudelaire's programmatic sonnet 'Correspondances' and many symbolist poets. It occurs is many passages in Proust's great noc vel as when he thinks the woods of Hudismenil have a message for him which, try as he might, he cannot decipher. The Russian poet Alexander Blok was obsessed with the notion of a woman behind whom lay the world secret.

I must say something about Frank's early life. As his name shows he was Italian and many English tradespeople had the greatest difficulty with his name, even desperately resorting to 'Coffee'. He was born in Vico Equense just south of Naples and near Sorrento.

Italy, like Russia, is not very productive of philosophers. Vico Croce and Gentile are the best known. I think Vico Equense may have been named after Vico, or possibly vice-versa. There was great poverty there and consequently mass emigration to the United States. Cioffi was brought up by his grandparents. His mother sadly had died in giving birth to him and after that his father had refused even to see him. He must have been a brilliant boy, but started skipping school around the age of fourteen. I suspect this was because it was not stimulating enough, for one of the reasons he missed school was so that he would have more time to read in the New York Public Library. He was conscripted just after the end of the war and served in Japan, a spell which he much enjoyed partly I suspect because Japanese girls afforded GI's in the swimming baths. At some time he had read the Japanese novel in translation and particularly recommended to me Tanizaki's *The Makioka Sisters,* a novel of family life somewhat akin to Jane Austen, and the very un-Austen like erotic novel *Some Prefer Nettles.* Fortunately, he was discharged from the army before the Korean war of 1949- 1951. He then spent some time in Paris where he became very friendly with the black novelist James Baldwin. Here again I suspect he availed himself of Parisian erotic life for I recall his rather typically observing to me that the anticipation as you ascended the stairs with the streetwalker was much more gratifying in the anticipation rather than the fulfilment.

Drawing on finance from the G.I. Bill of Rights and with the help of Alan Bullock he then entered Oxford to read PPP Philosophy, Psychology and Politics. We overlapped at Oxford but though I suspect we may have both been in the Kemp café then popular with lecture dodging students who had missed breakfast through sleeping in. Frank was one of the editors of *Cherwell* which along with *Isis* was one of the two student newspapers. I believe the later newspaper proprietor Rupert Murdock was their financial adviser. He also very much favoured having tea in the famous covered market which joined the High Street and the Turl.

He had for a time the redoubtable Anscombe as a tutor. At the time she was engaged in translating Wittgenstein's *Logical Investigations* and sometimes she would suggest he look through the proof sheets on the table. Word of this got round among the philosophers which at that time had more philosophers to the square mile than anywhere else in the world, and so Frank became much sought out by them. He was also taught by Anthony Quinton and by that sad genius Friedrich Waismann. Waismann had been a friend of Wittgenstein and a member of the Vienna Circle. At first Wittgenstein had been pleased by the thought that Waismann was writing an exposition of his philosophy, but then harshly changed his mind about the project. When Frank went to Waismann's house the door was opened by his melancholy son who later tragically committed suicide.

Frank had a strong interest in sociology. He recommended Max Weber and Adolf Schutz's work to me, in particular Alfred Schutz's insightful *The Phenomenology Of The Social World*. At the time the work on institutions and on human interaction of Erwin Goffmann was very much in fashion. Frank raised the question of whether Goffman's work gave us knowledge, Did he not just point out what we already knew in a way the novelist does? One is reminded of the old joke that a sociologist is a man who can't find his way to a brothel without consulting a PhD on prostitution.

Frank then went on to a post in philosophy in Singapore. Here he met his future wife Nalini to whom he dedicated his collection of essays on Freud. Her father had been the manager of a rubber plantation in Malaya. When the Japanese came they were notorious for their cruelty, beheading anyone who offended them. As it happens a Japanese general stopped to rest at the plantation and had tea there. He then posted a notice to the troops in Japanese saying that they were not to be disturbed. This was very fortunate for them. But unlike Frank Nalini could not bear the Japanese for many years afterwards. Sadly Nalini became ill and bedridden and died shortly before Frank had his fatal fall on the stairs.

As the university expanded to four colleges, Eliot, Rutherford, Keynes and Darwin, Frank moved to each while I stayed put in my room in Rutherford. But in the early 1970s when the University of Essex opened he was invited there to be the professor of philosophy as founder of the philosophy department. He was to make all new appointments in philosophy. He had also to weather the storm of much greater student unrest than in Kent. I visited him when I could and gave a paper on Karl Loewith and Nietzsche's second untimely meditation on the uses and abuse of history entitled *On the uses and disadvantages of history for life*. He appointed David Farrell Krell who, to his disappointment I think, became a devotee of the deconstructionist Jacques Derrida. More sympathetic was Nick Bunnin. Nick had a Chinese wife and often visited China. He was interested in German Idealistic philosophy. We became friends and when he moved to Oxford after he retired, I used to visit him and we had many pleasant discussions. Frank was succeeded as head of department by the neo-Kantian Onora O' Neill who came from a famous Ulster family.

And now I must come to three other philosophical friends two of whom it was my good fortune to meet, Peter Hacker, Rahim Hassan .I only got to know Anthony Daniels through his books printed under the name Theodore Dalrymple

It was a lucky day when the philosophy department at Kent invited Peter Hacker to give a series of seminars and public lectures on the philosophy of Wittgenstein. I used to meet him at the station. We would lunch together and he came to the house and met my wife Barbara whom he very much admired.

He was a fellow of St Johns College Oxford, and we sometimes visited him in his flat there. On one or two occasions I had lunch with him in college.

Peter was famous for his commentaries on Wittgenstein's notoriously difficult *Philosophical Investigations*. This work was to give rise to a form of philosophical analysis different from that practiced by Russell and Moore. It was to become known as connective analysis. In using it, the analyst traces the complex ramifications of philosophical concepts. It was to be practiced by Peter Hacker, Peter Strawson, Georg Hendrick Von Wright in his *Varieties Of Goodness*, Bede Rundle in his dissection and dissolving of the problem of existence in *Why Is There Something Rather Than Nothing*, and Herman Philipse

Peter Hacker rejects the Quinean view that philosophy is continuous with science in trying to articulate the truth about the nature of things. For Peter the task of philosophy is to explore the Kantian and Wittgensteinean problem of what it is meaningful to say, what Strawson in the title of his book on Kant called *The Bounds Of Sense*. Some aspects of this seem paradoxical at first to the layman. For example most people would assent to the proposition that I know what I am feeling, but I don't know what you are feeling. But this is confused. Once we see that the concept of knowledge is correlative to the concept ignorance in that you can't have knowledge without the possibility of error then it is clear that this dichotomy does not hold about one's feeling pain. 'You can have another person's pin, but you cannot have another person's pain' is not a statement of empirical fact, but a grammatical rule. One of the pleasures of philosophy is exploring the labyrinths of thought that philosophers can get lost. Descartes created many of them with his assumption that we can only know our ideas and that we can therefore doubt the existence of a world outside them. Yet it was Descartes who wisely observed that there is no idea so absurd that some philosopher has not put it forward. *Mea culpa'* he should indeed have cried. In his criticisms of the neuroscientists who confuse the brain with the person and thinking with the state of the brain Peter Hacker has shown how scientists who step outside their specialist empirical investigations slip into talking nonsense. Von Wright in his book *The Varieties Of Goodness* showed in a manner analogous to that of Aristotle that the predicate 'good' does not point to the single essence Plato had aspired to discover, but is used in a variety of ways. To use a facetious example a good cricketer is not necessarily a good man for technical goodness differs from moral goodness. Of course all cricketers hope that cricket, unlike football say, is a school of moral goodness.

Peter has produced a splendid tetralogy *The Conceptual Framework*, *The Intellectual Powers*, *The Passions* (the eighteenth-century word for the emotions) and *The Moral Powers*. In the latter he draws on some poems of mine for illustration. In his wide reading of both history and literature, helped in his case by his multi-lingualism which enables him to quote Hebrew and Classical Greek, he resembles my friend Frank Cioffi. Frank, however, was, as they say, not versed in the tongues. Fortunately Freud had been well translated. Peter's tetralogy should be read by anyone interested in philosophy.

I now come to the remarkable Rahim Hassan. Rahim studied physics at the University of Baghdad where that remarkable television commentator on science Jim Al-Khalili also studies. As one attended in the day and the other in the evening they never met. Rahim left Iraq because of the murderous dictator Saddam Hussein. I did not meet him when he taught physics at Kent. After his retirement he settled near Oxford and founded a discussion group which met every Wednesday from 4 p.m. to 6 p.m. in a café in the Jericho district of Morse fame. This had now become gentrified since my undergraduate days where students only visited it because the cinema there specialized in foreign, particularly French, films. Every month the contributions to *The Wednesday* were published online. They were then collected and produced for sale in beautifully printed volumes with fine art work. There are now over a dozen of these. The past discussions of literature, history and philosophy are all available online at www.thewednesdayoxford.com. Rahim has been a great stimulus to my investigating many topics in English and European literature and in history and philosophy and has published many of my poems.

Finally I must come to Anthony Daniels who has published many books under the pseudonym Theodore Dalrymple. I have never met him in person, but only through his books. In 2019 he produced a book about literary references on the part of English and American poets from Akenside to Carlos Williams. It was called *Illness As Inspiration*: *The Poetry Of Medicine And*

Disease. Strangely enough my old tutor Freddy Bateson had once remarked that the writing of poetry has often supervened on a feeling of sickness on the poet's part. In it Anthony referred very favourably to my poems of grief at my son's suicide. We then got into contact by email.

As a doctor he had travelled widely in Africa and Asia, but claims that he has never come across such cruelty and depravity as in England even in the worst civil war situations. This is because he worked as a prison doctor in England and saw the worst of men. In *The Knife Went In* published in 1918, a phrase murderers often use, his opening chapter tells a terrible story of cruelty in which a woman was also involved as a perpetrator of violence. The murdered man had borrowed £10 so that he could buy drink. When he did not pay the money back the result was horrifying. I quote 'The victim, besides being an alcoholic, was disabled, close to heart failure, and able to move to and from his electrically-reclining chair only with difficulty. That made it easier to torture him. They broke his legs, they broke his ribs (all of them), they fractured his skull. They boiled kettles and poured the water over him. Still no £10.' Not surprisingly he died within the hour. He goes on to say that the woman felt no guilt because she had only been a bystander. In fact he grew quite to like her when she had been sobered up by being in prison. She even expressed horror when he told her about a woman who had stabbed three men to death, commenting: I don't know what this world's coming to.' A nice twist in a horrible take! Of course the book acknowledges that some murderers are quite beyond sympathy citing the case of a man who had impaled three babies on railings because they had made too much noise. He could never be brought to see that he had done wrong. Men who cannot understand the language of morality rapidly begin to use it when they feel that they have been wronged.

Theodore, as I will call him in this section, maintains that so called 'cold turkey', withdrawal from heroin, is not as difficult as is often made out. He regards forced intimacy and the lack of privacy as worse than solitude. The inertia of the police, so well known to complainants about crime is mentioned.

In *Second Opinion* (2009) the loss of a historical frame of reference is seen as a disaster for a culture. Meeting a young man who does not even know when the Second World War occurred he discovers that the young man does not know a single date.

In *Not With A Bang* a topic much in the news now, that of murderers who kill again when they have released, is discussed in the chapter *Real Crime, Fake Justice*. It makes one feel that the Probation Service should be abolished. This book was published in 2009.

But enough of the dreadful world Theodore Dalrymple has so vividly portrayed and let us come to Anthony Daniels, the man behind the pseudonym. He must be one of the most widely read and cultivated men it is possible to meet.

24 A SAD AND MOST DISILLUSIONING EPISODE IN AGE

It will already have emerged from this book that I have always had a keen interest in the pleasures of sex. Unlike Sophocles as described at the beginning of Plato's *Republic,* I regard it as good fortune that my potency has persisted well into age, for as I write this I am 87 much to the surprise of the people to whom I announce the fact. But potency is demanding and requires an outlet and I dislike solitary masturbation.

My wife Barbara's protracted lung disease made her very weak and, of course, put an end to what had been our very lively sex life. Even at its height that did not satisfy me, however, for I sought variety in mature girls and women. Man, as William James pronounced under the influence of laughing gas, is naturally polygamous. Barbara had had the experience of finding out her happily married brother frequented pornography. She was a woman of the world and adopted the very enlightened attitude of saying to me that she did not mind what I got up to as long as I did not tell her about it. She did not want a repentant male melodramatically grovelling at her feet.

After Barbara' death I went into a period of acute isolation and disorientation. It was the time of the 2019 General Election, so I tried to throw myself into local politics, going to meetings which the candidates addressed and asking questions.

I felt acutely lonely because my son had not yet moved down from his work in Birmingham to live with me and work from home. I also spent much time in Zoom discussions with my own literary group and with two philosophical groups, one in Oxford and one in Canterbury. Nevertheless the need for a physical relationship with a woman gnawed at me. I went on dating sites and I also discovered the strange world of 'escorts'. This is made up of young and pretty girls from Spain, German, Italy and Eastern Europe and the Far East who advertise their services online through paying agencies to put their enticing photographs and details online with their phone numbers. It is a strange world. There will be at least forty of these girls in quite a small town advertising their services locally. When you call their numbers their phones are often out of service, presumably because they have moved elsewhere or gone home. Sometimes they work in a rented house or flat in pairs, sometimes singly. Though they are fulsome in the services they offer online some of them are surprisingly distant and reluctant when you speak to them and if you do get a meeting the reception is often not quite as advertised. Nevertheless I came to admire the courage of these girls. Firstly they had left home for a foreign country. Secondly, apart from some of the oriental girls, they had acquired fluent English and often spoke a third or even fourth language beside their own as well. Thirdly meeting strange men can be a dangerous game. There is always the risk of robbery or even murder.

One evening some time in March 2020 I went to a small flat in the town where I live, Canterbury. It was very near the fourteenth century West Gate. I was very nervous. I rang the bell. The door opened, but as is usual in such encounters the girl stood behind the door so as not to reveal her deshabille to anyone passing in the street on which the door opened directly. From behind the door, the girl, whose face I had only momentarily caught a glimpse of, pronounced the word 'Hello' in a most enchanting and enticing tone. Once inside the hall I saw one of the most beautiful girls I have ever met. She had the dark skin of the south, lovely eyes and smile and beautiful long black hair. Her figure was perfectly proportioned with lovely breasts and slender waist. She had plump beautifully shaped buttocks which I found particularly attractive. Very strangely, however, and, somewhat disconcertingly, she had tattoos on her arms and waist and upper limbs. She led me into a small room on the left whose curtained window gave out on the street from which I had just entered. It was a ground floor flat. The room contained a double bed. As I sat on it and undressed I asked her about the tattoos. She said she had had them done in memory of her brother who had died in the railway station in Barcelona, the city from which she came. It was uncertain as to whether his death had been suicide, but she thought that suicide was more likely than an accident and, indeed suicide seemed likely to be the verdict of the forthcoming inquiry. Suicide at a railway station immediately brought to mind *Anna Karenina*, my favourite novel. Her brother had been a couple of years or so older than herself and something of a thinker. His favourite philosopher was the same as mine, Nietzsche. He had been particularly impressed by aphorism 574 of *Daybreak:* 'The higher we soar, the smaller we seem to those who cannot fly.'

All this and the fact that my younger son Edward had also committed suicide made her seem sympathetically close to me as well as sexually attractive. I had always romanticized Spain and its literature. I had started Spanish at school with the French master Mr Lawton whom I idolized. Many years ago I had even read *Don Quixote* in the original Spanish. My favourite Spanish poem is the 'Noche Oscura' of San Juan de la Cruz. I would bring *The Penguin Book of Spanish Verse* to our meetings and recite it to her. I particularly relished the line '*Amado en la amada trasformada*'. But Sophia had her surprises for me right from the start of the affair. She later told me that she was Romanian and that both her parents (who were schoolteachers) had come to Spain from Romania. Her first language was in fact Romanian and so her second language, Spanish, was not perfect. She did not know much about Spanish Literature and seemed pleased to learn about it from me. I tried, not very successfully to learn some Romanian which, although it is like Spanish and Italian descended from Latin, is much more difficult.

I wrote a poem about my impression at the start of the affair. The title 'Strange Encounter' will recall to those of my generation that so very British film with Celia Johnson and Trevor Howard 'Brief Encounter'.

You waited for me for our strange encounter,
Young, lithe and supple at my anxious greeting,
The bed was ready as it was so often,
With you not knowing whom you would be greeting.

So sweet you were and strange, ready to talk
Of anything I wished to talk about,
Your mode of life, your lack of catholic faith,
Of what you still believe, of what you doubt.

For you still felt some hand has set us here,
We're animals, but beyond Darwin's scope
Each of us has a right to their belief:
You were absorbed by what the mystics hope.

*The fragrant south had bred your lissom body
So ready for each act that I desired,
Ready for talk, ready for caresses,
Ready to slake the thirst desire inspired.*

*You'd not believe there's no life after death,
You spoke about the mystics you had read,
I wondered what you found in them to be
So sure that we live on when we are dead.*

*Bought charms can still be charms, and your strange life
Seemed one of courage yet, somehow so sad,
A stranger among strangers with no friend,
Just the succession of the men you'd had.*

*Soon you would go home, this world forgotten,
Though you'd still exercise, read mystic books
In Barcelona. Gone this strange existence
Of trading for a while upon your looks.*

*A personality shone through the acts
That you performed, a warmth, a delight
Beyond your sweet ingenuous youthfulness:
Your innocence shone through so clear so bright.*

*We said goodbye, agreed to meet again,
I was enrolled among your clientele,
I'd been afforded all that I desired,
What future though? That only Time would tell.*

*What do you feel about me now we've met,
Indifference perhaps, or tenderness?
What thoughts were hidden by your lovely face?
Although I gazed at you I could not guess.*

Your brother may have been a suicide
As was my son. We probed the mysteries
Of family life, your loves and your dislikes,
Both of us formed by different histories.

And then, the end for which I had been driven
To enter once again your rented room,
We held each other in the tight embrace
Voluptuaries proclaim life's finest bloom.

You gave me sex with real tenderness
And yet it seemed that love was still held back,
Though love cannot be bought, perhaps you tried,
Yet in my ecstasy I felt its lack.

Once more I felt the coming longed for spasm
Poured out in all the bliss that I could find,
I groaned and fell back drained from what must be
The greatest pleasure known to humankind,

Alas not mutual in this encounter,
Though tenderly we kissed and said farewell,
I stepped into the cold and dark outside
Still held by what we'd done as by a spell.

Did you go back to studying mysticism
Or pliantly await another's lust?
I hoped, despite that, you'd somehow be blest,
And yet this world of ours is rarely just.

A strange encounter, but not brief maybe,
Although Rachmaninov might be our tune,
What does the future hold for you and me?
Our secret meetings may be over soon.

You want to go back to the world you know
And may your future bring you what you've willed,
Although I wish you did not wish to go
My greatest wish is your wish is fulfilled.

    I went to her flat every Saturday and sometimes on a weekday as well as spring approached. We talked about Spain and literature and history and suicide, for, as Camus said, suicide is the central problem of philosophy, Hamlet's 'To be or not to be'. Before sex I would sit on her bed, reading 'Noche Oscura' which I was trying to learn by heart, or a poem or piece of prose I myself had written. I gave her the early part of this autobiography in which she expressed a sympathetic interest. She told me she was paying to do a correspondence course in nutrition. Even I could not fail to notice that she was always talking about the expenses some project incurred. She told me that her ambition was to open a café in Barcelona. That would involve considerable outlay. I promised to give what help I could financially. I wrote a poem about the café which pleased her greatly. She told me that she was going to frame it and put it on the wall.
    Then she recounted a complicated story of criminal intrigue the truth of which I shall never know now she has left me. About two years before, young and ambitious and wanting to get rich quick so she could lead the high life, she had agreed to be a drugs courier. She obtained the drugs from a dealer, but, in some complicated way, she was robbed of them without payment either by another criminal or the intended recipients. This meant she was in debt to the dealer for about £20,000. If she did not pay some unspecified dire consequences would ensue. She might be hurt.

Her parents might be told of the way of life she was leading and they too might be hurt physically. In addition she told me that she had gone off to live in Italy for a time with a young Italian crook. What she said to her parents about that escapade I do not know. Whether it had any connections with the other affair I do not know either. I should have remembered the old saying that one cannot touch pitch without being defiled. It was on this trip that she learned to speak Italian.

It was in this way that she began to acquire sums from me far in excess of what I paid her for her sexual services. I had cashed in £30,000 from premium bonds I and my wife had bought and donated that sum to Hertford College for an annual prize and bursary in my late wife's name for students there. As by now Covid had started in earnest and she claimed that it was running her into even more expenses because of the enforced closure of her café, I informed the college that I needed part or whole of the money to help a friend in business difficulties because of the Covid epidemic. The college generously agreed to return the whole sum.

Sophia, as she called herself (all escorts work under false names), was in Barcelona struggling (as she claimed) with both the problems of the café and the payments to her blackmailer. I missed her greatly. An adviser at the bank became worried by the amount of money I was paying into her account. Then she said she had got Covid and we could only speak with difficulty over the phone when she managed to get out into the hospital garden.

She seemed delighted to meet me and be together again when I met her in the dusk at Canterbury bus station after her return from Barcelona. She never liked train travel, perhaps as a result of her brother's death at a railway station. She embraced me spontaneously and warmly and we went to her flat. She did not like to come to my house because she knew my friends and my son distrusted her.

One day when I went to the bank to transfer yet more money to her I was surprised to be called to the office of a customer adviser. I was still more surprised to find two policemen waiting for me in his office. They had been told of the sums going out of my account and suspected what they called a 'love trap', a phenomenon apparently very familiar to them. When I told Sophia about this she was very worried. Eventually we went to the police station together. By chance there was a lost Romanian young lady there being helped by a young English couple. Sophia seemed to show her good nature here by spontaneously helping with translation as the girl spoke no English at all. We were then interviewed by the police both together and separately and the police decided not to pursue the matter.

Sophia had had to go back to the continent on several occasions. Hoping to raise money she said she had had to work in brothels in both Germany and Switzerland, but had not been able to earn much as the brothels were in small towns and consequently had a small clientele. I was still sending her money to make up for this and ran into further expense by booking provisionally trips to see her abroad.

At last she returned. At Christmas she went back to Spain and she phoned me to tell me her blackmailer had met her and said he was now satisfied with what she had paid and would not trouble her any more. She expressed great gratitude to me for my help in freeing her from this burden. She said she would always remember what I had done for her and how good I was.

The end came abruptly and shockingly in June 2021. I had been paying £800 a month for the upkeep of her flat. We went there and she made love passionately and she seemed to share the pleasure fully and spontaneously.

But she announced that she was leaving the flat abandoning escort work and going to live in London. She intimated that she would meet me there, but gave no address. We would keep in touch by email and mobile phone, she said. She was much more adept at using than the mobile phone than I was. She claimed she had started working as a telephone receptionist for an employment agency which, again, she was careful not to name.

At the same time she said she was studying an expensive course on laser treatment for cosmetic surgery for women who wanted it. She said such treatments could be expensive for a client. A facial improvement operation could be as much as £800. She also told me that she was going out with a young man, an engineer.

Everything seemed fine and she agreed to meet me for lunch at an Italian restaurant in central London. We discussed our situation and she gave every sign of wanting to go on meeting periodically in London. She did not wish to travel to Canterbury any more.. The weather had been sunny and hot for days, but on the Friday when we met it was cloudy and wet .I walked with her back to Green Park tube station through a romantic mist. There were swans on the Serpentine and as we crossed a bridge we could see Buckingham Palace faintly outlined in the distance. She gave me every sign of continued affection in our farewell embrace. It was Friday June 4 2021. She then cut off all email and mobile phone communication and, it seems, has disappeared from my life forever. I conclude with a bitter poem 'The Dupe' which this experience has prompted.

THE DUPE

How could I know, bowed down beneath Love's yoke,
That you embodied what the playwright named:
'The smiler with the knife under the cloak',
As cold, as unashamed?

I was so far entangled in your net,
I gave you all the money I could find,
And then you cut me off with no regret,
Ungrateful and unkind.

Even to give you much of what you took
I called back aid to others I'd agreed,
When with a troubled and a plaintive look
You spoke of pressing need.

Oh how you duped me, cunning, crafty, cool,
While I was foolish-fond, clay in your hand,
I see now how you played me for a fool,
I try to understand,

But can I? No. I find your icy heart
Rooted in coldness far beyond my scope,
Even when it came the time to part,
You roused in me false hope

You loved me still. With you it was no crime
To take more money from me when we met
For what you'd planned would be the final time:
You'd go without regret.

You had found something you could do with ease,
You'd praise my goodness, express gratitude,

*Knowing how such flattery would please,
And with delight, delude.*

*You wrote the play and played your role so well
Assigning me my pitiable part,
So I became the victim of the spell
Of one who has no heart.*

25 ON POETRY AS CONSOLATION

I must now speak of the role poetry has played in my life. I can best express it by saying with Wordsworth that poetry for me is

A joy, a consolation and a hope.

There are three kinds of poetry, epic, lyric and tragic, the latter combining elements from both, for it includes both narration and lyric. The father of all poets is, of course, Homer. I have tried to learn enough Greek to understand the invocation to the muse which opens *The Iliad*. My favourite lyric poet is Sappho with her renowned ode '*Phainetai moi*' in which Sappho says that the man in front of her seems to be a god because he is gazing at the beautiful girl she loves. It has been translated into many languages, the translation into Latin by Catullus being the best known. It shows that, as Peter and Ursula Dronke pointed out, C.S. Lewis was quite wrong in saying the cult of love originated with the troubadours in the middle ages. My favourite tragedians are Sophocles and Shakespeare.

It is curious that the final and shortest line in a Sapphic ode ends as did the Homeric hexameter with a dactyl and a spondee, a long and two shorts and two longs in classical languages and, in modern stressed languages, a stressed syllable followed by two unstressed ones and two stressed ones as in the Sappho poem which ends '*koma katairei*'. The English phrase 'And sleep falls slowly' might illustrate this.

I have spoken earlier of the tragic vision as replacing religion in helping us to come to terms with death. When Nietzsche saw the falsity of all religions and the impossibility of a theodicy, I think he saw this reconciliation to mortality as the function of tragedy. As I said earlier his view influenced both F. R. Leavis and my tutor Freddy Bateson. The German classical scholar Kurt Von Fritz showed in his wonderful book *Tragische Schuld Und Poetische Gerechtigkeit, Tragic Guilt and Poetic Justice* that Aristotle's notion of *hamartia* has often been misinterpreted. It does not mean a character flaw on the part of the protagonist, but a mistaken decision which leads to disaster. Moreover in tragedy, contrary to the neo- classic interpreters of Aristotle such as John Dennis, the virtuous are not rewarded and the bad punished. Socrates and Jesus are untragic figures.

Poems which express feeling are not liked by modern editors who represent the sophisticated *literati* of today. I recently wrote a poem 'Winter Funeral' in classical hexameters. It goes:

Is not winter the best time for funerals
When half of nature is dead, no leaves on the trees,
And no birdsong is heard from the wood?
The sun is bright above the gathering mourners
The coffin is lifted on sturdy shoulders,
It bears a mind once patiently thoughtful,
A person who loved to converse about books,
One who has now reached the end of her own story.
So let us say farewell to the one we loved to see
Patiently waiting her turn to speak wise words.

My favourite English lyric poet is Andrew Marvell with his balanced poem about Cromwell and his pastoral poems about the garden at Appleton House the Yorkshire home of the general commanding the parliamentary army, Lord Fairfax. Marvell was private tutor to his daughter Mary.

I have translated into English poems from French, Spanish, German, Russian and Italian. These were Baudelaire's 'Correspondances' Guillen's *'Muerte a lo Lejos'*, Nietzsche's *'From High Mountains'* Pushkin's 'I Loved You Once' Tiutchev's *Silentium*, Blok's *'The Unknown Woman'* Dante's sonnet *'La Donna Mia'* and Leopardi's 'L'Infinito'.

I conclude with the famous choric ode 'Polla ta deina' 'Many are the wonders' in the *Antigone* of Sophocles lines 332-375 in which the tragic poet gives the best perspicuous representation of the earth and the place of human life within it. The ode is on pages 134-135 of E.F.Watling's Penguin translation. I like it, but I would point out that the use of the words 'evil' and sin' gives a too Christian tone. As Nietzsche argued we should replace these with the concepts good and bad, the concepts the Greeks used. I was shocked to learn from Edith Hall's introduction to the World's Classics edition that the performance of Sophoclean drama was generally proscribed on moral grounds by the Lord Chamberlain. The ode runs :

Wonders are many on earth, and the greatest of these
 Is man, who rides the ocean and takes his way
Through the deeps, through wind-swept valleys of perilous seas
 That surge and sway.

He is master of ageless Earth, to his own will bending
The immortal mother of gods by the sweat of his brow,
As year succeeds to year with toil unending
Of mule and plough.

He is lord of all things living; birds of the air,
Beasts of the field, all creatures of sea and land
He taketh, cunning to capture and ensnare
With sleight of hand;

Hunting the savage beast from the upland rocks,
Taming the mountain monarch in his lair,
Teaching the wild horse and the roaming ox
His yoke to bear.

The use of language, the wind-swift motion of brain
He learnt; finding out the laws of living together
In cities, building himself shelter against the rain
And wintry weather.

There is nothing beyond his power. His subtlety
Meeteth all chance, all danger conquereth.
For every ill he hath found its remedy,
Save only death.

O wondrous subtlety of man, that draws
To good or evil ways! Great honour is given
And power to him who upholds all his country's laws
And the justice of heaven.

But he that, too rashly daring, walks in sin
In solitary pride to his life's end.
At door of mine shall never enter in
To call me friend.

26 ON MY SON MATTHEW

I want to conclude this memoir *Past and Present* by speaking of my son Matthew. I have already spoken in the earlier parts about his life as a boy. Now, as I approach ninety, he has entered his sixties. I don't quite know what to make of this fact. Matthew has always wanted to be independent, never to be a burden. Despite his physical and educational setbacks he was determined from the age of fourteen to get a job. He would try anything. He once worked in a tanning factory where the manual lifting required was so heavy that he had to leave. He worked on a farm. He worked as a baggage handler at Manston airport. He worked on a farm in Chartham.

He was quite prepared to travel to get a job and found one upgrading distributors for old cars in a small firm in Brierley Hill to the West of Birmingham. He paid for a small flat there. I was always anxious when he had to drive from Birmingham to Canterbury, peering through the curtains to see the lights of his car in the drive. One day, after my wife's death, he was driving my trusted old Polo of fourteen years and was hit by a Hungarian lorry on the M26 which only has two lanes. The Hungarian driver was high up on the right side of the cab and did not see him. The polo was knocked into the central reservation and a total wreck, but fortunately Matthew stepped out of it unhurt. The insurance was risibly small £400. Matthew got that much for selling it as scrap.

Matthew had paid for the upkeep of a small flat there. He had always loved cars and at weekends he went to motor races as a marshal. These included the famous Le Mans Twenty-Four Hour race where marshals came from Holland and even the U.S. When he went to America he visited his fellow marshal Nancy from Atlanta. Later he became a member of a rescue and first aid crew and his ambulance is even now stationed in our drive.

As I recounted earlier it was very fortunate that he was with the rescue unit nearby at Lyddon when Barbara died and so he was with me at the very moment of her death. He could see that I was completely shattered and disorientated and prepared to do all kinds of strange things for company. He talked to his boss and his boss kindly agreed that he could set up a workshop in our garage and work from home. The materials would be sent from Brierley Hill and then returned by courier when finished and he would be paid by piece work. The arrangement is still working well.

Matthew has a loving, cheerful and optimistic temperament. He puts up with all my temperamental vagaries which are not a few. In particular I suffer from what the French call *'lubies'* or odd eccentricities. They arise because I have OCD, Obsessive Compulsive Disorder. This takes the form of being mysteriously forced to perform certain rituals. I try to keep this hidden, of course, but when someone is as close as Matthew he is bound to observe them. Fortunately he is more amused than irritated by them.

Let me give some examples. I have to enter a room in certain ways. If there are books in it I have to focus on a certain author as I walk in, Clarendon in the downstairs sitting room and F.R. Leavis when I enter the upstairs living room. I also have to look across at the cathedral tower after having done this. When I touch walls I have to wipe them afterwards as though they are contaminated in some way.

Like Dr Johnson I have to step across lintels and boundaries in pavement stones without touching them. I have to wash my hands frequently. I also have number superstitions. Unlike the Pythagoreans I regard not the even, but the odd numbers as unlucky. I must aways purchase two or multiples of two of whatever I am buying, whether books or tins of soup. Because my brother Bobby was shot down and killed when he was 23, I have to wash my hands whenever I reach page 23 of whatever book or paper I am reading. Of course I can't alter my date of birth, December 23 1933. Matthew's nickname for me is 'the worry-wart'.

Fortunately we have a wonderful lady, Katie, who does our cleaning and washing, coming in once a week. Matthew however does all the supermarket shopping. His own swallowing difficulties mean he has to have soft ready made meals such as fish pie or cottage pie, but he can cope with fish fingers and chips and, his favourite, fried eggs and bacon. The latter I cook, the former he puts in the oven and then serves. Every night at eight o'clock we have what we call the happy hour, two small Cointreaus and four chocolates each. Matthew has become very fond of reading the crime novels of Agatha Christie and also of reading books about her, and those of an American mystery writer called Ivanovich, so I always know what to buy him for a present. We never quarrel over the television. Both of us are particularly fond of programmes about history, in particular the intriguing ones by Lucy Worsley. Matthew has bought a new car which, perhaps wisely given my age, he does not allow me to drive. He often saves my having to pay for taxis, however, by driving me and we are hoping to travel to Germany and Italy in the summer. As well as doing all the food shopping at the supermarket he tends the garden and mows both front and back lawns.

'What would I do without him?' is the question I often ask myself.

Perhaps my feelings about him are best conveyed in a poem which I wrote some time ago:

TO MATTHEW
Matthew is working in the shed,
Soon I will call him in for tea,
Such simple things, let it be said,
The best of what it means to be.

Both cheerful in the Autumn sun
Walk in the garden which he tends,
His work, I hope, will soon be done
For pleasures that the evening sends:

The TV talking and our dinner,
And then we'll both be off to bed,
I tell him that he should be thinner,
We both discuss the books we've read.

Where can there be a greater pleasure
Than fathers in their sons can find?
Each in the other finds a treasure,
Two bodies, but a single mind!

27 IN MEMORY OF MY DEAREST BARBARA

How better to conclude this autobiography than with an account of the many virtues of my late wife Barbara. As I described earlier I was first struck by her physical beauty. The more I got to know her I was pierced by the sense of her moral beauty, especially when I consider all the vicissitudes which she had to face. I cannot to better at this point than to quote Wordsworth and say that she was

'A perfect woman nobly planned.'

She loved reading, music and the arts. Indeed as regards art she was my *cicerone*. She had done an art history course at the Open University after we were married and worked hard though she was burdened with family cares as I have described earlier. So when we visited Florence and Venice she pointed out to me the beauties of many works of painting, sculpture and architecture. The baptistery doors of the *Duomo* in Florence by Ghiberti, the departure from the Gothic style in Alberti's Ospedale Delle Innocenti and Donatello's very effeminate looking David in the Bargello museum. She also pointed out many frescoes to me and named and discussed their painters. She had a deep knowledge of Ruskin, including his multi-volume *The Stones Of Venice*. When we looked at the columns of the Doge's palace she said that John Ruskin's drawings were so detailed that it would be possible to reconstruct the building from them if it were ever destroyed. She loved Italy deeply. Italy's splendid monuments of art were what we missed most in New Zealand. Its lovely landscapes did not compensate for the lack.

No wonder so many New Zealanders take the trip to Europe, and Italy in particular. I met many who were studying Italian for that purpose. We used to take Matthew in his pram into Hagley park, gaze at the lovely Cashmere hills, but long for Europe.

Barbara also enjoyed meeting my German friends in Jena, Jochen and Gudrun Sander. Gudrun's daughter Kirstin later visited us in Canterbury. Barbara was in awe of the forest in Thuringia and interested to see the Wagner house in Bayreuth with its strange motto: 'Wo meine Wahnen Frieden Fand__Wahnfried__Sei Dieses Haus von mir benannt' 'Where my woes found peace__Wahnfried__ may this house be named' which I translated for her. She thought the Nietzsche houses in both Naumburg and Weimar places of sorrow. I could not bring her to share my admiration for this greatest of philosophers.

Barbara loved visiting France. We visited the cathedral at Amiens spurred on by Ruskin's book about it. We explored Flaubert's Rouen and the area of the country where George Sand was born and lived. Barbara loved being in Paris,

She worked hard to improve her French and tried to read French authors in their native language. She explored with great interest and enjoyment the work of women writers who came from North Africa and wrote in French.

Barbara had a keen interest in music. She was always trying to improve her piano playing. We had the good fortune to go to many recitals, concerts and operas. These included hearing Beethoven's late quartets when we were in Oxford and Tchaikovsky's *Evegeny Onegin* conducted by Gergiev in Paris and both *Siegfried* and *Lohengrin* in Berlin with that wonderful Berlin opera chorus. The *tremolo* in the overture to *Lohengrin* played on the violins set both our hearts quivering.

We both greatly admired Dmitri Khvorostovsky's singing of Rachmaninov from when we saw him at the Cardiff song contest. Alas he died so young. Polonsky's poem '*Vchera mi stretilis* ' 'Yesterday we met' which towards the end has the line '*Na vechnuyu razliku proschai*' ' For an eternal parting farewell'. She loved Marcel Proust's friend and lover Reynaldo Hahn's settings of French poems and the wonderful four last songs of Richard Strauss particularly the last one '*Abendrot*' 'Evening' which was played at her funeral. It ends with words reminiscent of the wonderful close of Swinburne's 'The Garden of Proserpine'

O weiter stille Friede!
So tief im Abendrot!
Wie sind wir wandermuede
Ist das etwa der Tod?

Oh wider stiller peace!
So deep in evening's glow,
How tired we are of journeying
Is this something of death?

Barbara had so bravely left her family and friends to voyage to a land 14,000 miles away, about the farthest inhabited place one could go. An evening tossed in the Bay of Biscay and in Cook Straits are experiences not to be forgotten, as I can assure you.

She always had a keen interest in education. She got a first for her Open University work and she also did a degree at the University of Kent with distinction. She was very interested in the work of D.H. Lawrence and obtained an M.A. for her thesis on Ruskin's influence on Lawrence. I have already mentioned how much we loved reading *War And Peace* and *Anna Karenina* together.

She had known so many joys and sorrows in family life and in her last years she suffered greatly from her immobility. At least she died peacefully in her home with her husband and son near.

I have never had Barbara's ashes scattered though I have often wondered whether to do so in the parks in North Oxford where we loved to walk. They were near where she lodged for so long, Park Town. But the urn still faces me as I lie down to sleep in my bedroom. Matthew and I have just decided that, when I die, he will scatter the ashes of both of us together in the river Isis as it flows under the bridge in the Parks.

I wrote a sonnet about the urn and ashes inspired by a memorable line from the Latin elegiac poet Propertius. It has been revised as I write as often happens with poets. As the Poet Paul Valery said to the critic Jacques Riviere, 'A poem is never finished':

A BURDEN THAT A SINGLE HAND CAN HOLD

'Sum quod quinque digitis levatur'

'I am a burden that five fingers lifts'

'A burden that a single hand can hold',
So wrote Propertius centuries ago,
And yet imagination makes this so
That in that casket lies not ash, but gold.

The grains of pure love cannot be counted,
A love her love of music could express,
A love unrivalled in its tenderness
A love whose height could never be surmounted.

Into such little space such riches packed,
Such memories compressed into one store,
Such deep devotion, honour, love and trust.

There you remain, life's warmth alone is lacked,
You somehow are, although you are no more,
If only love could give life to your dust!

I wrote the following poem which I read at Barbara's funeral:

IN MEMORY OF BARBARA ANN GREENWOOD 1933-2019

I think of all the life's that's there outside
As through the curtains comes the whitening dawn,
And down the windowpane the raindrops glide
As showers green the lawn.

Two nights ago you slept here by my side,
Breathing with labour, but, waking, a bright mind.
Only a day has passed now since you died,
And bonds still strongly bind.

Alone in bed I conjure up the past,
All the vicissitudes of life we shared,
But every life in death must end at last,
So yours could not be spared.

They came to carry your remains away,
With all the reverence we owe the dead,
For husband and for son a bitter day,
And more such days ahead.

As life must end, so must a piece of verse,
Although I would prolong it if I could
In the called for endeavour to rehearse
All that you did of good.

But thankfully so many of your friends
Join here to mourn the treasure they have lost,
We know we all must bear what nature sends,
Though heavy is the cost.

Poets are vain, let me put pen aside,
Sit and think silently on life, on death,
But speech is stubborn and won't be denied,
Breath mourns the end of breath.

And reason too comes to assist the heart,
And thinks it right to give a voice to pain,
When those who love hear strike the hour to part
And never meet again.

THE ENVOI OR COMMIATO FROM THE LAST TWO VERSES OF SWINBURNES 'THE GARDEN OF PROSERPINE':

From too much love of living,
From hope and fear set free,
We thank with brief thanksgiving
Whatever gods may be
That no life lives for ever;
That dead men rise up never;
That even the weariest river
Winds somewhere safe to sea.

Then star nor sun shall waken,
Nor any change of light:

Nor sound of waters shaken,
Nor any sound or sight:
Nor wintry leaves nor vernal,
Nor days nor things diurnal;
Only the sleep eternal
In an eternal night.

Very appropriate sentiments for a man approaching ninety!

Appendix

IN MEMORY OF MY ENGLISH TUTOR
F.W.BATESON
FOUNDING EDITOR OF ESSAYS IN CRITICISM

(This poem was originally published in the journal he founded *Essays in* Criticism in April 2023).

I wish I could have given you this book,
My book of poems written since you died,
Now I recall those days, when, at your side,
I read, and looked up while your kindly look

Suffused the room with calm, and Merton's bells
Chimed every quarter through the afternoon.
Ah, how that hour was over far too soon,
As England's poets wove their magic spells.

It seemed you were a father to me then,
For, in my first term up, my father died.
If only those times could come back again

And I had then my verse, as I have now,
To read to you, and you'd hear it with pride
And speak of it as only you knew how.

My two sons Matthew and Edward